The People's Bible Teachings

CHURCH—MISSION—MINISTRY

The Family of God

Armin W. Schuetze

NORTHWESTERN PUBLISHING HOUSE
Milwaukee, Wisconsin

Library of Congress Card 95-71845
Northwestern Publishing House
1250 N. 113th St., Milwaukee, WI 53226-3284
© 1995 by Northwestern Publishing House.
Published 1995
Printed in the United States of America
ISBN 0-8100-0577-8

Table of Contents

Editor's Preface

The People's Bible Teachings is a series of books on all of the main doctrinal teachings of the Bible.

Following the pattern set by The People's Bible series, these books are written especially for laypeople. Theological terms, when used, are explained in everyday language so that people can understand them. The authors show how Christian doctrine is drawn directly from clear passages of Scripture and then how those doctrines apply to people's faith and life. Most importantly, these books show how every teaching of Scripture points to Christ, our only Savior.

The authors of The People's Bible Teachings are parish pastors and professors who have had years of experience teaching the Bible. They are men of scholarship and practical insight.

We take this opportunity to express our gratitude to Professor Leroy Dobberstein of Wisconsin Lutheran Seminary, Mequon, Wisconsin, and Professor Thomas Nass of Martin Luther College, New Ulm, Minnesota, for serving as consultants for this series. Their insights and assistance have been invaluable.

We pray that the Lord will use these volumes to help his people grow in their faith, knowledge, and understanding of his saving teachings, which he has revealed to us in the Bible. To God alone be the glory.

Curtis A. Jahn
Series Editor

Introduction

The sign along the road reads: Trinity Ev. Lutheran Church, corner Pine St. and 2nd Ave. As you approach this corner, you see a large brick building identified by an imposing tower with a cross on top. Clearly this building is the church to which the sign directs.

The signboard in front of the church announces: Sunday School and Adult Bible Study—9:00 a.m. Worship Service—10:15 a.m. James Smith, Pastor. WELCOME.

From this sign you conclude that Trinity Ev. Lutheran Church is more than the building you see. People go to church here and do church work. A pastor serves the people and works in the ministry of the church. Since the church calls itself *Lutheran*, it must belong to a church body that is Lutheran.

A dictionary may list as many as nine different meanings for the word *church*. It can mean a building, a place of worship, the service itself, a congregation, a denomination, or all Christians taken together.

Our concern is to see what the Bible means when it speaks of the church. What does the church do? What assignment has God given the church? Through whom does the church carry out its assignment? We will direct our attention to these questions as we look at *the church, its mission, and its ministry*.

Part I

The Church

1

The Church: What do you mean?

When the Bible speaks about the church, it is talking about people. The word used in the Greek (*ekklesia*) means a gathering or meeting, or more literally, a group of people who have been called out or brought together.

The Bible speaks more particularly of the "church *of* God" (Acts 20:28; 1 Corinthians 1:2; and many other references). This is a group of people who belong to God or have been gathered together by God. That is the church according to the Bible.

The family of God

Who are the people whom God has brought together and calls his church? The apostle Paul gives the answer: "You are all sons of God through faith in Christ Jesus"

(Galatians 3:26). All those who, through faith in the Lord Jesus, have become children of God are the church of God. They are also called the "family of God" (1 Peter 4:17) and the "family of believers" (Galatians 6:10). In fact, this family extends beyond the people now living on earth. They are called the "whole family in heaven and on earth" because God is their heavenly Father (Ephesians 3:15). The Lord Jesus also called the members of this family his brothers and sisters (Matthew 12:50). He teaches them to call God in heaven "Father" (Matthew 6:9).

The church—what a blessed family! What a privilege to be a member of this family, to call the almighty God our Father, and to have Jesus as our brother! What a privilege to have many, many brothers and sisters who have all been called together by God into his family for time and for eternity!

The temple of God

This church is not a building. Yet Scripture uses the very apt illustration of the church as a building, a spiritual building. The apostle Paul assures the Gentile believers that they too are "fellow citizens with God's people," that is, with the Jewish believers, God's chosen people in the Old Testament times. They are all "members of God's household." Paul then goes on to describe the church as a building. The church is "built on the foundation of the apostles and prophets, with Christ Jesus himself as the chief cornerstone. In him the whole building is joined together and rises to become a holy temple in the Lord. And in him you too are being built together to become a dwelling in which God lives by his Spirit" (Ephesians 2:19-22).

Picture this building to yourself and your part in it.

Important to any building is its foundation, which must be firm and solid, unshakable. The "apostles and prophets" are the foundation on which the temple of God is built. This refers not to them as human beings, but to the Word they wrote by inspiration. The writings of the apostles and prophets, the Scriptures of the Old and New Testaments, are this foundation.

When Peter, in behalf of all the apostles, confessed, "You are the Christ, the Son of the living God," Jesus said he would build his church on this rock, on the truth about Christ which Peter had confessed. Even the gates of hades (hell) would not overcome it (Matthew 16:16,18). There is and can be no other foundation: "For no one can lay any foundation other than the one already laid, which is Jesus Christ" (1 Corinthians 3:11). Accordingly, in this foundation Jesus Christ himself is the "chief cornerstone." He is the very center of the Holy Scriptures; they "testify about me," Jesus said (John 5:39). Remove Christ Jesus from the Scriptures, and they become meaningless.

On this foundation the church is built. People are brought to faith in Jesus. As believers, and only as such, they become building stones that are built together on the foundation. Each believer is another brick or building stone that forms part of "the holy temple" as it rises on the foundation of the Christ-centered Word. By faith in the Lord Jesus as your Savior, you became one of those building stones in this spiritual building, the church.

By calling the church the "holy temple in the Lord," Paul designates the building he has described as "a dwelling in which God lives by his Spirit." When Old Testament Israel was commanded to build the tabernacle and then the temple, God was present there, in the Holy of Holies, the innermost part of the temple. In the New Testament, Paul tells the believers in Corinth, "We are the temple of the living God" (2 Corinthians 6:16).

What a marvel the Lord is revealing to us! What a privileged position he is giving all believers! We, together with the believers of all time, make up this spiritual building in which God himself, the Father, Son, and Holy Spirit, dwells. This temple of God, built up of all believers, is the church.

The Lord is the builder

Like every building, this spiritual building, the church, has a builder. He is none other than the Lord himself. Jesus told Peter, "I will build my church" (Matthew 16:18). The Bible tells us about the church that had been founded in Jerusalem on the day of Pentecost: "And the Lord added to their number daily those who were being saved" (Acts 2:47). Yes, it is the "church of God." It is built by him and belongs to him. How the Lord does this will be considered in a later chapter.

The body of Christ

Another expression the Bible uses in speaking of the church is "the body of Christ." This too shows how closely believers in the Lord Jesus are bound to one another and to the Lord Jesus. Paul calls the church the "body" of him who is its head, the Lord Jesus (Ephesians 1:22,23). He writes to the Romans, "In Christ we who are many form one body, and each member belongs to all the others" (12:5). The various members of the body need and serve one another with their differing gifts as directed by the head. From Christ, the head, "the whole body . . . grows and builds itself up in love, as each part does its work" (Ephesians 4:16). How close we are to one another in the church as members of the "body of Christ," dependent on one another and totally under the direction and control of our loving head, the Lord Jesus! How we should love him and our fellow believers in this spiritual body!

Known to God

The church is made up of those who, through faith in the Lord Jesus, have become part of God's family, the church. It consists of believers. But how can we know who is a believer? Since we believe with the heart, we would have to look into another person's heart to know for certain if that person is a believer. That, however, is totally beyond the ability of any human being, and to attempt to do so is presumptuous, like playing God. We can look at the "outward appearance," but only "the LORD looks at the heart" (1 Samuel 16:7). Faith in the heart is not for man to see, so only the Lord, "knows those who are his" (2 Timothy 2:19).

Invisible but real

For this reason the church, consisting only of believers, can be called invisible. This is not to say that the believers who make up the church are invisible. The faith in their hearts, however, is invisible to us, so it is impossible for us human beings to gather together into one outward church body all believers and exclude all hypocrites and unbelievers. We, therefore, cannot identify the church of God with any one denomination, because it extends into all denominations. There are, for example, Lutherans, Catholics, Baptists, Presbyterians, Methodists, and Episcopalians who believe in the Lord Jesus as the Savior from sin. Yet, the exact identity of each believer remains unknown to us. In that sense the church of believers remains invisible to us.

Nevertheless, the church is not a phantom, an invisible product of the imagination. It consists of real people, who live and labor in this real world. We see them and live and work with them. But only God knows who is truly a believer and a member of his spiritual family. In the next chapter we will consider where and how God makes it possible for us to find his church here on earth and be a part of it.

Luther's description

In his Large Catechism Luther explains the words of the Apostles' Creed, "communion of saints." In doing so, he gives a simple, clear description of the church. He writes:

> The Creed calls the holy Christian church a *communio sanctorum*, "a communion of saints," . . . To speak idiomatically, we ought to say "a community of saints," that is, a community composed only of saints, or, still more clearly, "a holy community." . . .

> This is the sum and substance of this phrase: I believe that there is on earth a little holy flock or community of pure saints under one head, Christ. It is called together by the Holy Spirit in one faith, mind and understanding.[1]

In the Smalcald Articles Luther says it simply: "Thank God, a seven-year-old child knows what the church is, namely, holy believers and sheep who hear the voice of their Shepherd."[2]

In contrast to the scriptural teaching confessed by Luther, Rome taught (and still teaches) that the church was the visible body that was ruled by the pope, who claimed to be the vicar of Christ. Thus, they claimed it was an outwardly visible body. Luther, on the other hand, "believed" in the church. He knew it not by sight, but by faith.

One holy Christian and apostolic Church

The Nicene Creed describes the church as "one holy Christian and apostolic Church." One—even though we see many church bodies and congregations in the world, there is only one church. This is the church the Bible speaks of as consisting of all believers of all time. This is the church Jesus founded.

This church is called holy, and the believers who make up the church are "saints." The apostle Paul writes to the "church of God in Corinth" as "those sanctified in Christ Jesus and called to be holy" (1 Corinthians 1:2). Through faith in the Lord Jesus, they have become saints—holy. Their sins have all been removed. "Christ loved the church and gave himself up for her to make her holy, cleansing her by the washing with water through the word, and to present her to himself as a radiant church, without stain or wrinkle or any other blemish" (Ephesians 5:25-27). As a believer you are a saint, not because of anything you have done, but because the Lord Jesus has made you a saint by cleansing you of all sin through his life, death, and resurrection.

The word that is translated Christian in the Nicene Creed, literally, is the word catholic. Catholic means universal. The one church is universal because it includes all Christians, everywhere, of all time. Since the word catholic was taken over into the name of the Roman Catholic Church, this word in the creed was translated "Christian." Wherever there is a Christian, one who believes in the Lord Jesus, that is where the church is.

The church is also called apostolic. As we noted earlier, it is built on the apostles and prophets. The inspired writings of the apostles and prophets are the foundation for all the church teaches and believes.

We also confess of this church in the Augsburg Confession: "one holy Christian church [that] will be and remain forever."[3] We already noted the words of our Savior that "the gates of Hades [hell] will not overcome it" (Matthew 16:18). Here on earth it will continue as the *church militant*. This means it will continue to be attacked by Satan. It needs to fight against all those who want to undermine the Christian faith and destroy the church. In heaven it continues forever as the *church triumphant*. There the saints triumph in perfect peace and glory with their Savior forever.

You and the church

You believe in the Lord Jesus as your Savior from sin. You can know that you are a member of the holy Christian church. The Lord Jesus is your head, whom you follow as the Good Shepherd. You can pray to God as your heavenly Father. You have many, many brothers and sisters throughout the world who care for you and pray for you as you do for them. And you have a host of brothers and sisters who already are in heaven—your first parents, Adam and Eve; Abraham; Joseph; David; Isaiah; Mary, the mother of Jesus; the apostles; and Luther, to name but a few. What a blessed family! Here on earth you cannot identify each family member by name; you cannot look into anyone's heart. But by faith you know they are there, united with you by a common faith, hope, and salvation through the precious blood of your Redeemer. And through faith in the Lord Jesus, you can be assured of a place with all the saints in the church triumphant in heaven.

2

The Church: Where can you find it?

The family of God—how wonderful it will be when this family has its grand reunion in heaven! Nothing is better than life with your heavenly Father and Jesus, your Savior-brother, together with all your Christian brothers and sisters, with all the believers who ever lived. What joy!

But you are still on earth. You know that you have many brothers and sisters in the family of God, the church, right now, here on earth. You would like to be with them also now and have a family gathering, a get-together with fellow believers. Since you cannot look into their hearts to identify them, how and where can you find your family of believers?

You remember the sign you saw along the road: Trinity Ev. Lutheran Church. You found the building on Pine St.

and 2nd Ave. and saw the invitation to worship. You went to the announced service, and many other people also were there. Since these people were meeting in a church building and called themselves a church, you said to yourself: This must be where I will find fellow believers; this is where I will find the family of God. But how could you be sure? Perhaps this gathering only called itself a church. Then the service began. You heard the pastor invite the people to worship in the name of the Father, Son, and Holy Spirit. You heard them confess their faith in the triune God. The pastor read and preached from the Bible. You remembered that Jesus once said, "Where two or three come together in my name, there am I with them" (Matthew 18:20). Jesus must be present here, you concluded, for these people are gathered here in Jesus' name. You said: I have found the church; I have found my Christian family.

Was your conclusion correct? Paul made a similar conclusion about the people gathered at Corinth who called on the name of the Lord. He addressed a letter to them: "To the church of God in Corinth, to those sanctified in Christ Jesus and called to be holy, together with all those everywhere who call on the name of our Lord Jesus Christ—their Lord and ours" (1 Corinthians 1:2). He called the people who gathered in Corinth in Jesus' name "the church of God."

The visible church

Paul wrote his letter to a visible congregation. It was in a certain place, Corinth. The letter could be handed to the members and read by them, a visible group of Christians. The same was true of the people with whom you worshiped at Trinity church; these were visible human beings. And you said of this visible assembly: Here is the church of God.

But hadn't we concluded that the church of God is invisible? Has it now become visible? Yes and no. It remains invisible in that you cannot say of every one of the several hundred persons gathered at Trinity church that they are believers; you cannot look into the heart of any one of them and see the faith that may or may not be there. But the church has become visible in that you can know with certainty that believers are present at Trinity. In that sense we can call a certain visible gathering a church, because of the believers who are there. That is what we mean when we speak of the visible church.

The means of grace

But what makes you so sure that believers are present? We have to ask the further question: What causes faith to grow in the heart? How does someone become a believer? As we answer this question, let us take the example of grass and rain. When it is dry, grass soon withers and dies. But when it rains, you know that the grass will turn green. It takes rain to make it grow.

The Lord uses this illustration to tell us what it takes for faith to grow: "As the rain and the snow come down from heaven, and do not return to it without watering the earth and making it bud and flourish, . . . so is my word that goes out from my mouth: It will not return to me empty, but will accomplish what I desire and achieve the purpose for which I sent it" (Isaiah 55:10,11). What does God want to accomplish through his Word? Paul gives the answer: "Faith comes from hearing the message, and the message is heard through the word of Christ" (Romans 10:17). We are to expect God's Word to be fruitful on the soil of the human heart, causing faith to sprout and grow. That is God's promise.

The Holy Spirit works by means of the Word. The same is true of the Sacrament of Baptism. Peter told the Pentecost assembly: "Repent and be baptized, every one of you, in the name of Jesus Christ for the forgiveness of your sins. And you will receive the gift of the Holy Spirit" (Acts 2:38). Through God's message that Peter preached and the Baptism the apostles performed, 3,000 came to faith, found forgiveness in Christ, and became part of the church at Jerusalem. Their faith was also strengthened as they broke bread together in the Sacrament of the Lord's body and blood (Acts 2:42). The gospel in Word and sacrament works and preserves saving faith in the human heart. That is why the Word and sacrament are called *means of grace*. They are the means the Holy Spirit uses to lead us to believe what God in his grace has prepared for us in Christ Jesus.

Effective means

When you visited Trinity church and heard the pastor read and preach the Word of God, you correctly concluded that believers were in this congregation. You even heard the people confess their faith. But perhaps they only spoke those words with their lips. Perhaps they did not really believe in their hearts. There may indeed have been hypocrites present who pretended to believe, but you could not know who they might be, nor should you try. You could, however, be sure that everyone was not a hypocrite. True believers were there. You could be sure of this because God's Word is effective.

Remember how Isaiah compared God's Word with rain and snow. It will accomplish what God sent it to do. The gospel is also called "the power of God for the salvation of everyone who believes" (Romans 1:16). Jesus says, "The words I have spoken to you are spirit and they are life" (John 6:63). Through the gospel, the Holy Spirit works the life of faith that leads to eternal life. The faith produced in the individual heart is invisible to us, but the gospel in Word and sacrament, which produces and preserves faith, is visible.

Given to believers

What is more, the Word of God would not be preached in a congregation of people if believers were not present. God did not entrust the preaching of his Word to the unbelieving world. He gave his gospel to believers, to his church. To Christians he said: "Go and make disciples . . . baptizing them . . . teaching them to obey everything I have commanded you" (Matthew 28:19,20). So if you see a gathering of people concerned about preaching and hearing the Word of God, as you did at Trinity congregation, you correctly conclude: Here are believers doing what Jesus commanded them to do.

Marks of the church

We have just seen from the Bible that the Holy Spirit works faith through the gospel, that the Word of God is effective, and that God has given his Word to the church to preach. For all of these reasons, the means of grace are called the *marks of the church*.

A mark is a means of identification. The word "flour" or "sugar" identifies what is in a certain jar. Similarly, the gospel as it is preached and heard assures us that believers are present in that gathering. We can be sure because of what God says about the power of the gospel. Thus it marks the presence of the church.

Because of the believers who are present, we call such a gathering marked by the gospel a visible church. Not that this is a church apart from and different from the invisible church. The one holy, Christian church, the communion of saints, is present in the visible congregation that you call a church. You are not mistaken in calling it the church of God, a family of believers. If hypocrites are present too, they are not part of the invisible church, even though they are associated with the outward assembly. In charity you will assume that all who confess their faith are sincere, and you will look upon them as brothers and sisters in Christ. If it should happen that the pastor is a hypocrite, the gospel he preaches and the sacraments he administers are still valid. His unbelief does not nullify God's promises.

The gospel alone

A building called Trinity Ev. Lutheran Church does not identify that place or the people who gather in it as the church. The fact that a pastor steps into a pulpit to preach to a group of people does not make it a church. If the pastor preaches what he has devised with his reason, if he is merely interested in preaching about good morals, if he expresses his views on politics, if he sets forth his own ideas about God, then his preaching is not a mark of the church. The church's presence is known only by the true Word of God, not by anything the pastor or anyone else may add, and certainly not by any errors that are taught. Only the true gospel and genuine sacraments are marks of the church.

Apology of the Augsburg Confession

We sum up what we have said with some quotations from the Apology of the Augsburg Confession, Articles VII and VIII.

> The church is not merely an association of outward ties and rites like other civic governments, however, but it is mainly an association of faith and of the Holy Spirit in men's hearts. To make it recognizable, this association has outward marks, the pure teaching of the Gospel and the administration of the sacraments in harmony with the Gospel of Christ.[4]

> Hypocrites and evil men are indeed associated with the true church as far as outward ceremonies are concerned. But when we come to define the church, we must define that which is the living body of Christ and is the church in fact as well as in name.[5]

> We are not dreaming about some Platonic republic, as has been slanderously alleged, but we teach that this church actually exists, made up of true believers and righteous men scattered throughout the world. And we add its marks, the pure teaching of the Gospel and the sacraments.[6]

> In accordance with the Scriptures, therefore, we maintain that the church in the proper sense is the assembly of saints who truly believe the Gospel of Christ and who have the Holy Spirit. Nevertheless, we grant that the many hypocrites and evil men who are mingled with them in this life share an association in the outward marks, are members of the church according to this association in the outward marks, and therefore hold office in the church. When the sacraments are administered by unworthy men, this does not rob them of their efficacy. For they do not represent their own persons but the person of Christ, because of the church's call, as Christ testifies (Luke 10:16), "He who hears you hears me."[7]

We took note of the joy it is to know that we are associated with Christians of all time in the holy Christian church, the communion of saints, and that we will be associated with them throughout eternity in heaven. It is likewise a source of joy to be associated with them in a visible assembly in which the gospel is rightly taught and the sacraments are rightly administered. By these marks we know that this is where we can find the church of the living God here on earth.

Various outward forms

When you attended divine worship at Trinity congregation, you liked what you saw and decided to take a closer look. You wondered whether it was the same as some other churches you attended.

You noticed that Trinity used a hymnal you had not seen before. The congregation followed a particular order of service, and some parts were different from what you had seen at other churches. The service folder informed you that Trinity had two pastors and a Lutheran elementary school with five teachers.

You visited one of the schoolrooms. The teacher started classes with a devotion, and the children studied the Bible and Luther's Small Catechism. From this you concluded that the church was present here too.

The congregation belonged to an association of congregations that conducted a Lutheran high school. In this school the Word of God was taught and learned, and devotions were held in Jesus' name. The marks of the church revealed the presence of the church also here.

You were told that this congregation was associated with a larger body that was called a synod. Many other congregations also belonged to the same synod, whose purpose was to work together in training pastors and teachers to preach and teach the Word of God, in sending out missionaries, and in publishing Christian literature. Here, too, the marks of the church revealed its presence.

As we look at the visible church, we see congregations, schools, synods, and various types of organizations. On the basis of the church's marks, we see the church present in each of them. The outward form of a congregation or Christian assembly or association may vary, but wherever the marks are in use, Christ and his church are present.

Some say that God has commanded Christians to form congregations and local churches, and that God instituted only this visible form of the church. Therefore, any other assemblies or associations of Christians, like synodical bodies, are only human arrangements. This position has been held by many in the Lutheran Church— Missouri Synod.

God does indeed command Christians to assemble. This is inherent in the command to teach and preach the gospel and to administer the sacraments. The early Christians recognized this (Acts 2:42). When some withdrew from their assemblies, they were admonished: "Let us not give up meeting together, as some are in the habit of doing" (Hebrews 10:25). Christians need the encouragement they can give one another. They need to "spur one another on toward love and good deeds" (v. 24).

This requires first of all some kind of local gatherings. Christians must gather at some particular place where they will regularly hear God's Word and receive the sacraments; where they are encouraged, admonished, and edified; where church discipline can be carried out according to Matthew 18. We call these primary gatherings local congregations.

God, however, neither prescribes nor describes in detail the "where" and "how" and the liturgical orders and the organizational structure of such local congregations. The early Christians no longer saw themselves bound by the many ceremonial laws of the Old Testament, which had prescribed in detail the temple building, the festivals and sacrifices and worship. Those were all commanded to foreshadow things to come. Once Christ had come, the shadows were replaced by "the reality," which "is found in Christ" (Colossians 2:16,17). Now Christians were directed to preach the gospel of Jesus Christ, to baptize, to administer the Lord's Supper, and to worship and praise God in prayer and song (Colossians 3:16,17). No formal ceremonial structure in regard to place or organization or order of worship was commanded. These could be determined freely according to what best served the gospel and the people of God.

In the interest of the gospel and of their mutual strengthening and help, the "assembling" of Christians also went beyond local meetings. The believers at Jerusalem and Antioch had close contact with one another. The church at Jerusalem sent Barnabas to Antioch, and he brought Paul from Tarsus (Acts 11:19-26). Both of them preached for a year at Antioch, and then this congregation sent them on Paul's first mission journey (Acts 13:2,3). When a dispute arose between some men from Judea and Antioch about the necessity of circumcision, representatives from Antioch met in Jerusalem with the apostles and elders to consult about this question (Acts 15:1,2,5,6). Later, congregations in Galatia, Macedonia, and Achaia joined in a collection to help the poor in Jerusalem (1 Corinthians 16:1-4). Thus on a wider scale too, the Christians freely "assembled" to spur one another on to faith and good works. Here, too, the church was present and functioning no less than in the smaller local gatherings in Jerusalem or Antioch or Corinth or wherever it might be.

Similarly today, Christians, who first of all are members of local congregations, may also join together as circuits, conferences, districts, and synods. Some of them may also join Lutheran high school associations or institutional mission societies. In all of these, Christians come together in Jesus' name to carry out the Lord's work. In all of these, the church is present.

Organizational structure

As we noted earlier, the particular organizational structure of congregations and also of church bodies and other church organizations is agreed upon in Christian freedom. God does not order this by law.

Already at the time of the Reformation, denominations were formed, partly because not everyone recognized this truth. The Roman Catholic Church had insisted, and still insists, that the pope, as the successor of Peter, must be recognized as the one visible head of the church, with a hierarchy of bishops to rule the church as the successors of the apostles. In opposition to Rome, the Episcopalians, Presbyterians, and Congregationalists adopted their own particular forms of church organization and government, and each denomination claimed divine institution for its form.

The Lutherans saw no divine mandate in Scripture for any one form of organization or church government. They were even ready to allow the bishops to "rule" the church, if only the bishops would permit the gospel to be preached freely and in all its truth. Congregations and church bodies could be organized in whatever way would best serve

God's people in their particular situation. Particularly in America, the church could freely organize without interference on the part of civil government. Lutheran churches, recognizing that all Christians are "kings and priests" (1 Peter 2:9; Revelation 1:6), have to a great extent followed democratic procedures. We will explain this priesthood of believers in a later chapter.

Love and good order

But if there are no divinely ordained ceremonial laws that determine how the church is to be organized and function, won't the result be chaos? Won't there be confusion and disorder as each congregation does what it pleases? Won't there be conflict between congregations? Won't an association of congregations, like a synod, try to dominate the individual, smaller group or congregation?

What will control the freedom God has given to his people? Paul wrote to the Galatians: "You, my brothers, were called to be free. But do not use your freedom to indulge the sinful nature; rather, serve one another in love" (5:13). This applies to each of us as individual Christians, and it applies to us also as we work together as groups of believers, whether as congregations or larger associations and synods.

Loving service does not ask: What will I get for myself? How can I exercise power over others and control them? Such attitudes indulge the sinful nature. Loving service asks: What can I do for you? How can I help you? How can I best serve and benefit you? Such questions will be the guiding spirit within a congregation. They will be the guiding spirit as congregations form associations to do the Lord's work. They will guide the relationship between a synod and its constituent congregations.

But what about avoiding confusion? The Corinthian congregation's worship had become disorderly. Paul describes the problem: "When you come together, everyone has a hymn, or a word of instruction, a revelation, a tongue or an interpretation" (1 Corinthians 14:26). When several people speak at the same time, no one benefits. Everyone thinks only: I have something to tell the others. No one is listening to anyone else. Paul advised them: "Two or three prophets should speak [one after the other], and the others should weigh carefully what is said. . . . God is not a God of disorder but of peace" (14:29,33). Paul concludes with the general directive: "But everything should be done in a fitting and orderly way" (14:40).

To facilitate good order, a congregation will adopt a constitution. By doing so, the members agree on how they will call a pastor, what officers they will have, their duties, etc. Congregations can agree on how they want to work together in a synod, and they can adopt a constitution and pass resolutions that provide for all things to be done in an orderly manner.

Where the gospel has done its work in the hearts of believers, the church will work together following God's will that all things be done according to love and good order. No divine laws regulate the organizational form and order of worship for God's people. In Christian freedom they may establish these as long as the Word of God is the only source in determining all matters of faith and life. The Augsburg Confession says, "It is not necessary that human traditions or rites and ceremonies, instituted by men, should be alike everywhere."[8]

Yet, love and good order may move congregations within a church body to strive for considerable uniformity also in such matters, and not selfishly assert their Christian liberty. In this manner they may wish to demonstrate the unity of faith that binds them together under God's holy Word.

3

The Church: How important is doctrine?

"It doesn't matter so much what you believe as long as you are sincere." "Churches don't all have the same teachings, but they all aim for the same goal: heaven." "There may be different roads, but they all lead to the same place." You may have heard words like these. They all give the impression that doctrine (what you believe and teach) is unimportant, that there isn't such a thing as true and false doctrine, that false doctrine does not really hurt anyone.

Destructive error

The devil would like us to believe that doctrine is not important. But remember, "he is a liar and the father of lies" (John 8:44). He deceives people into spreading his lies. The Bible calls these people "false apostles, deceitful workmen, masquerading as apostles of Christ" (2 Corinthians 11:13). Paul warns Titus against the "many rebellious people, mere talkers and deceivers" who "are ruining whole households by teaching things they ought not to teach" (Titus 1:10,11). Truth comes from God, but error has the devil as its father and is taught by false teachers, deceived by Satan.

Error is as dangerous as it is deceptive. It can ruin "whole households," whole congregations, and even church bodies. Paul was concerned about what the false apostles were doing to the Corinthians: "I am afraid that just as Eve was deceived by the serpent's cunning, your minds may somehow be led astray from your sincere and pure devotion to Christ" (2 Corinthians 11:3). Error does not build faith; it destroys faith.

Testing doctrine

Since error is so dangerous, we must ask, How can it be recognized? When a bottle contains poison, the government may insist that the label clearly say so. Teachers of false doctrine, however, do not label their doctrine as such. In fact, most often they will offer their product as wholesome spiritual food, even claiming support from the Bible.

Are we helpless against such deception? John gave his readers this advice: "Dear friends, do not believe every spirit, but test the spirits to see whether they are from God, because many false prophets have gone out into the world" (1 John 4:1).

But how is one to test what is taught? John advised them: "This is how you can recognize the Spirit of God: Every spirit that acknowledges that Jesus Christ has come in the flesh is from God, but every spirit that does not acknowledge Jesus is not from God" (vv. 2,3). What is taught about the Lord Jesus is of special importance. Do they teach that Jesus is both true God and true man? That in him "all the fullness of the Deity lives in bodily form" (Colossians 2:9)? That he gave his life on the cross as the one sufficient sacrifice for the sins of the whole world? That he bodily rose again from the dead? In other words, do they teach exactly what the Bible teaches about Jesus? Do they hold to all teachings of the Bible as Jesus commanded?

The Bereans tested even Paul's teaching by examining "the Scriptures every day to see if what Paul said was true" (Acts 17:11). But to be able to do such testing, you must know the Scriptures; you must read them regularly and examine them carefully. Scripture must be allowed to mean what it says and not be interpreted to mean what our reason would like. Jesus assures us: "If you hold to my teaching, you are really my disciples. Then you will know the truth, and the truth will set you free" (John 8:31,32). The Holy Scriptures, used honestly and with integrity, enable us to know the truth, to recognize error, and to distinguish true and false prophets.

Denominations and their confessions

Trinity congregation called itself Lutheran. Another has Presbyterian in its name; another Methodist, Baptist, Roman Catholic, or one of many different designations. Are these churches all alike? Do they differ in name only? How can we distinguish one denomination from another? Don't they all claim to teach what the Bible teaches?

To escape this difficulty, some congregations call themselves nondenominational or a community church. They do not identify with any denomination. They want to serve all people without asking them to commit themselves to anything besides the Bible, or faith in Jesus, or simply faith in God. What they, in effect, are saying is that what you believe is your private affair, that one denomination's teachings may be no better than another's, and that identifying with a particular denomination creates unnecessary division among Christians. This makes them look charitable, humble, and nonjudgmental.

But as we saw, God does want us to distinguish between truth and error. Among denominations we must distinguish between those that teach the truth and those whose teaching includes error. How can we do this? We need to examine their confessions.

What is a confession? Paul wrote to the Romans: "For it is with your heart that you believe and are justified, and it is with your mouth that you confess and are saved" (10:10). A confession reveals verbally what we believe in our hearts.

Jesus once asked his disciples: "Who do you say I am?" Peter, speaking for the disciples, was quick to answer: "You are the Christ, the Son of the living God." He expressed in spoken words what they believed about Jesus in their hearts. They made their confession, and it was a good one. Jesus gives the reason: "This was not revealed to you by man, but by my Father in heaven" (Matthew 16:15-17). What the disciples believed and confessed was not based on human philosophy and wisdom. What they confessed they had learned from God. What we believe and confess must be learned from the divine Scriptures in order to make a good confession that accords with the truth.

Just prior to asking the disciples for their confession, Jesus had asked them: "Who do people say the Son of Man is?" The answers varied: "Some say John the Baptist;

others say Elijah; and still others, Jeremiah or one of the prophets" (Matthew 16:13,14). What the people confessed about Jesus was false. It was based on their own thinking and expressed their human opinions. When one's belief and confession about God, Jesus, and salvation have their origin in the human mind, they will be false. Sinful human beings cannot know the truth about God except by revelation.

Thus, their confessions help us distinguish denominations from one another. Religious groups that have the Apostles' Creed (they may also include the Nicene and Athanasian creeds) as their confession will be considered Christian. They confess the true God as triune, and, in the Second Article, they confess the gospel of forgiveness in Christ. Those who fail to make even such a limited confession are not within the pale of Christianity. The marks of the Christian church are totally absent.

In addition to the above three creeds, Lutherans also express what they believe in the confessions contained in the *Book of Concord*. In these confessions they express with greater detail the various doctrines of Holy Scripture and reject teachings that are false. Similarly, other denominations may have their particular written confessions. We can and must test these statements of faith by comparing them with the teachings of Holy Scripture. When we do this, we will find that the Roman Catholic confessions fail because they do not ascribe salvation to the grace of God in Christ Jesus alone; instead, they assert that our works contribute toward gaining eternal life in heaven. They also contain teachings not found in Scripture at all but based on the traditions of the church. The various Protestant or Reformed confessions may err in what they say about original sin, or about Jesus and what he did for us, or about the role of good works in Christianity, or about Baptism and the Lord's Supper.

We must, however, not only test the written confessions. We must ask further questions: What do you mean when you call the Apostles' Creed your confession? What do you as a Lutheran mean when you say that you accept the confessions in the *Book of Concord?* What place does your written confession have in your teaching and preaching?

Answers to these questions may not be the same even within the same denomination. Take the Lutherans as an example. The Wisconsin Evangelical Lutheran Synod (WELS), on the one hand, "accepts the canonical books of the Old and New Testament as the divinely inspired and inerrant word of God and submits to this word of God as the only infallible authority in all matters of doctrine, faith and life . . . The synod also accepts the confessions of the Evangelical Lutheran Church embodied in the Book of Concord of 1580, not insofar as, but because they are a correct presentation and exposition of the pure doctrine of the word of God."[9] By accepting the confessions in the *Book of Concord,* the Wisconsin synod says that all the doctrines confessed in them were not revealed by any man, but by the heavenly Father in his holy Word. That is why the synod and its congregations require that all teaching and preaching correspond to these confessions. When you attended Trinity Ev. Lutheran Church, the pastor's sermon was based on the Scriptures and was in agreement with the Lutheran Confessions. The same is true of all congregations that are members of WELS. The same is also true of the Evangelical Lutheran Synod and its congregations, which are in fellowship with WELS.

Why isn't it enough simply to promise to teach and preach according to the Holy Scriptures? The problem is that false prophets also make that claim about their false teachings. When Wisconsin synod congregations require their pastors to teach and preach according to the Lutheran Confessions, they are telling their pastors that they expect them to teach Scripture faithfully, without changes and additions made by man. So we test both the written confessions and their public teaching and preaching. Do both agree with Scripture?

Accepting the Scriptures and the Lutheran Confessions, however, does not have the same significance for all Lutherans. The Evangelical Lutheran Church in America (ELCA), the church body that includes about two thirds of America's Lutherans, can serve as an illustration of this. Regarding Scripture, ELCA says: "This church accepts the canonical Scriptures of the Old and New Testaments as the inspired Word of God and the authoritative source and norm of its proclamation, faith and life."[10] While this statement sounds good in what it says, what is lacking is any reference to the Scripture's inerrancy. This was a conscious omission, allowing for a critical examination of what the Scriptures say, as we shall see.

ELCA "accepts" the Lutheran confessions with these words: "This church accepts the Unaltered Augsburg Confession as a true witness to the Gospel. . . . This church accepts the other confessional writings in the Book of Concord, . . . as further valid interpretations of the faith of the Church."[11] What is lacking is any commitment to the confessions as to their doctrinal content in all teaching and preaching.

This is a limited "acceptance" of the Scriptures and the Lutheran Confessions. This can be seen from what may be taught and preached in ELCA. The above "acceptance" does not prohibit a pastor or professor from preaching and teaching that the Bible has errors in it, that Adam and Eve may not have been real people, that evolution may be as true as the scriptural account of creation, that the virgin birth of Jesus is a myth, that Jesus' body never rose physically, and that some can be saved without believing in Jesus' work of redemption. Such teachings, and many more could be cited, are permitted in ELCA. Thus, to test the confession of a church, we must look not only at the official written confessions, but also at what is meant by "accepting" them and at what is acceptable teaching from the pulpit, in the classrooms, and in its periodicals and published writings.

We can test the churches and denominations on the basis of their confessions. We can distinguish between true and false visible churches, between those who confess the truth of Scripture in their confessions and are committed to it in what they teach and preach, and those who include or permit error in their confessions and in their teaching and preaching.

Fellowship

Why are we to test a church's or denomination's doctrine? Because God wants us to be associated with a visible church that teaches the truth and to stay away from those who teach falsely.

God wants to bless us through the Christian fellowship we practice with those whose confession is firmly based on Scripture. In the letter to the Hebrews, we receive this solemn encouragement: "And let us consider how we may spur one another on toward love and good deeds. Let us not give up meeting together, as some are in the habit of doing, but let us encourage one another—and all the more as you see the Day approaching" (10:24,25). God wants us to associate with fellow believers and to meet with them. Practicing Christian fellowship can be a rich source of encouragement as we live in a troubled world and as we face the devil's temptations. How eagerly we Christians should want to "carry each other's burdens" (Galatians 6:2)!

God has given Christians the best means with which to encourage one another. Paul wrote to the Colossians: "Let the word of Christ dwell in you richly as you teach and admonish one another with all wisdom, and as you sing psalms, hymns and spiritual songs with gratitude in your hearts to God" (3:16). What joy and encouragement it is for Christians to hear the Word of God read and preached in their churches and to sing psalms and hymns with their fellow Christians! What a blessing when that Word is a daily part of the family's life! What gratitude will fill the Christian's heart to the God who blesses and encourages us and supports and strengthens our faith in this way!

The value of belonging to a group that can provide support in troubled times is generally recognized. A close-knit family, a group of faithful friends, and people who have experienced similar problems can provide helpful support when needed. In the family of God we have a very special support group, one which the Lord Jesus has equipped with his word of comfort and wisdom, with the gospel that sustains faith. As members of this family, we are told to "encourage one another and build each other up, just as in fact you are doing" (1 Thessalonians 5:11). That is the very thing we are doing as we practice Christian fellowship with those whose confession is true to God's holy Word.

On the other hand, the Lord wants us to keep away from false churches, from those whose confession identifies their false teaching. Jesus warns: "Watch out for false prophets" (Matthew 7:15). John, the apostle of love, wrote: "If anyone comes to you and does not bring this teaching [the teaching of Christ], do not take him into your house or welcome him" (2 John 10). We are not to practice Christian fellowship with them or support them in their work. Paul urges us "to watch out for those who cause divisions and put obstacles in your way that are contrary to the teaching you have learned" (Romans 16:17). He says, "Keep away from them." That means, Do not practice Christian fellowship with them. Do not invite them to preach to you. Do not celebrate the Lord's Supper with them. Do not join with them in Christian worship.

God also tells us *why* he wants us to stay away from them. With their false teaching they "are not serving our Lord Christ." What is more, "by smooth talk and flattery they deceive the minds of naive people" (Romans 16:18). John also points out that by supporting a false prophet one "shares in his wicked work" (2 John 11).

The subject of Christian fellowship is not generally understood in today's world, not even in the Christian or religious world. The true significance and blessing of Christian fellowship is not appreciated, and the seriousness of false doctrine is not recognized. Some would even question whether any teaching that claims to be Christian can be called false or wrong. Not joining in worship and prayer with someone is considered uncharitable and judgmental. Suffice it to say here, in our practice of Christian fellowship, Scripture calls on us to distinguish clearly between true and false visible churches. Because of the importance and scope of this subject, a separate volume in this series is devoted to a more detailed study of fellowship.

Conclusion to Part I

"I don't need the church. I can worship God better just by myself." "There are so many different churches. It's all so confusing. How should I know which one is right?" "People who go to church are hypocrites. They think they are better than anyone else, but look how they live during the week!" For most people the church has little appeal. Most mainline denominations are declining in number even though the world's population is experiencing rapid growth. Organized religion, as some refer to the church, is often held up to ridicule by the media, by comedians, and even by educators. Our society worships pleasure, sex, science, wealth, health, the human ego—creation rather than the Creator. It rejects absolutes and all claims of having the truth. Such a society finds the church with its divinely inspired Bible inhibiting and confining and out of touch with today's world.

Jesus, however, continues to build his church. People are brought to faith through the gospel of forgiveness as it is preached and taught. Jesus also gathers Christians into visible churches and church bodies. He does not want each Christian to be alone in this world of temptations and evil. He wants us to associate with those who confess the truth of his Word and avoid those who pervert it by following human reason and desires. The Savior speaks these words of reassurance: "Do not be afraid, little flock, for your Father has been pleased to give you the kingdom" (Luke 12:32).

Part II

The Mission of the Church

4

The Church: What is its assignment?

When you moved to Centerville, you immediately decided to join Faith Ev. Lutheran Church. Why? What did you expect this church to do for you? Did you hope that membership at Faith would help your business? Did you expect that you would immediately acquire status in the community? Why did you want to be a member of Faith congregation?

The primary question, however, is not what *you* expect the church to do for you. We need to ask: What assignment has God given to the church; what does *he* expect the church to do for you? And then also, what does he expect of you as a member? Jesus gives the answer.

The Great Commission

The church, as we noted, is the gathering or congregation of believers. What assignment has God given to Christians as they continue in this world? Jesus said to his disciples before he ascended: "Go into all the world and preach the good news to all creation" (Mark 16:15). In somewhat greater detail, Matthew records Jesus' commission to his disciples: "Therefore go and make disciples of all nations, baptizing them . . . and teaching them" (28:19,20). Jesus himself would no longer be visibly present on earth to teach people. Now his disciples were to "preach the good news."

It is important to make good news known. When a new medication is discovered, this good news must be widely published so that as many people as possible may benefit from it. To hide its healing power from those who could be helped is heartless, if not cruel. So it is with the good news Christ commanded his believers to preach.

The book of Acts records how the disciples carried out this assignment. They acted as individuals. When the church in Jerusalem suffered persecution, "those who had been scattered preached the word wherever they went" (Acts 8:4). They acted also as groups of believers. The church at Antioch, for example, sent Paul and Barnabas on their mission journeys (Acts 13:2,3).

Teach—preach

The "good news" is a message the world needs to hear. This requires communication. The church, Christians, are to speak, tell, proclaim, teach, and preach. The church's commission has to do with words, God's Word as we have it in the inspired Scriptures.

The church has been assigned to teach "everything" Jesus commanded, including all the teachings found in the Bible. That is what Paul did. He could say, "I have not hesitated to proclaim to you the whole will of God" (Acts 20:27). This means not adding anything to Scripture nor taking anything from it.

Not every teaching of Scripture brings us "good news." The law, though it is good and perfect, is not good news for us. It reveals sin and proclaims judgment. What the Bible teaches about the devil, original sin, hell, and eternal damnation is not good news because we are sinners. Much that the Bible teaches sinners is such bad news that people deny that it can be true.

But wasn't it "good news" Jesus commissioned the church to preach? Should we forget about preaching the law? Should we forget about telling people about the devil, hell, and judgment? This is not what Jesus said to do, yet how can we preach the "good news" and still preach "everything he commanded"? Doesn't "everything" include the bad news?

The answer is that the bad news must be taught for the sake of the "good news," or the gospel. "It is not the healthy who need a doctor, but the sick" (Mark 2:17). The diabetic who believes himself to be healthy will turn away from the doctor who tells him to take insulin. The "good news" of forgiveness in Christ is indeed good news, but not until the law has revealed our sin. The good news is foolishness to those who consider themselves "healthy." As a result, Paul, who told the Corinthians, "I resolved to know nothing while I was with you except Jesus Christ and him crucified" (1 Corinthians 2:2), had to proclaim "the whole will of God" and show them their sin. Both sin and grace are included when the good news is preached.

The two basic teachings in the Bible are the law and the gospel. It is vital for the church to recognize this in its teaching. Both must be taught in close relationship with one another, but also with a clear distinction between the two. The purpose of each must be carefully recognized in their use. This is so important that a separate volume in this series concerns itself with these two teachings.

The church's commission to "preach the good news" includes the administration of the sacraments. When Jesus commanded his disciples to baptize, this was good news because God has given Baptism as a "washing of rebirth and renewal by the Holy Spirit" (Titus 3:5). When Jesus gave the church the Lord's Supper to distribute, this was good news because the body and blood, which the individual receives, give personal assurance of the Lord's forgiveness, purchased "with his holy, precious blood and with his innocent suffering and death."

Furthermore, the church's commission to "preach the good news" includes promoting good works. But doesn't Scripture say that we are saved "by grace . . . through faith . . . not by works, so that no one can boast" (Ephesians 2:8,9)? Because Lutherans stress salvation by grace alone, apart from works, they have been accused of teaching that good works are unimportant. Some have even said that good works are harmful to salvation. However, that is not what the Bible teaches and what the church must teach.

The church must promote good works because they are a necessary fruit of faith. We expect a good fruit tree to bear good fruit. In the parable, the fig tree that did not bear the expected fruit was to be cut down (Luke 13:9). Only trees that bear good fruit keep their place in an orchard; fruitless trees will soon become firewood. Since "faith without deeds is dead" (James 2:26), fruitless "Christians" do not retain their place in the family of God. The lack of fruit shows that they are spiritually dead.

But what are good works? What is good fruit? How is it produced? Only branches that are attached to a good trunk will produce fruit because the sap that keeps the branch alive and fruitful reaches it through the trunk. Jesus made this application: "I am the true vine. . . . No branch can bear fruit by itself; it must remain in the vine. Neither can you bear fruit unless you remain in me. I am the vine; you are the branches. If a man remains in me and I in him, he will bear much fruit" (John 15:1,4,5).

By faith Christians are attached to Christ, and from him they receive the strength to bear fruit. The unbeliever, cut off from Christ, can bear no fruit. Believers realize that "it is God who works in you to will and to act according to his good purpose" (Philippians 2:13).

The kind of works the Christian will produce corresponds to the will of God as revealed in his holy law, as we know it in the Ten Commandments. What is contrary to God's law is not produced by faith, but by a person's sinful nature. So the gospel is the fuel that keeps the Christian's motor running; the law is the road map that shows him which direction to go.

The church must promote good works as fruits of faith. This is part of teaching "the whole will of God."

Civic righteousness

Your neighbor is not a Christian. Neither he nor his wife go to church, but they are good neighbors. When you were sick, he mowed your lawn, and she does volunteer work at the local hospital. They are both active in making your neighborhood crime free. They are performing many "good works." However, because they are unbelievers, the works they do are not fruits of faith. The "good" they do is called "civic righteousness." Our confessions distinguish between such external works and the fruits of faith.

We read in the Formula of Concord:

> The distinction between works is due to the difference in the individuals who are concerned about living according to the law and the will of God. For as long as a person is not reborn, lives according to the law, and does its works merely because they are commanded, from fear of punishment or in hope of reward, he is still under the law. . . .

> But when a person is born anew by the Spirit of God and is liberated from the law (that is, when he is free from this driver and is driven by the Spirit of Christ), he lives according to the immutable will of God as it is comprehended in the law and, in so far as he is born anew, he does everything from a free and merry spirit. These works are, strictly speaking, not works of the law but works and fruits of the Spirit.[12]

Outwardly what the believer and unbeliever do appears to be the same. Both faithfully pay their taxes: the one, fearing the penalty for "cheating"; the other, because this is the will of the God who redeemed him. Both donate blood or contribute money to the Red Cross to help victims of a disaster: the one, looking for praise, expecting help in return in a possible time of need, or perhaps only desiring the reward of feeling good about himself; the other, as a fruit of faith, serving Christ in his neighbor. This is not to say that God does not also desire civic righteousness, outward obedience to the law. To promote this, God has established civil government. Government exists "to punish those who do wrong and to commend those who do right" (1 Peter 2:14). Thus it maintains law and order.

The mission of the church vs. the mission of government
We must remember that the mission of the church is distinct from the mission of the state. Both the church and state are institutions of God. Each, however, has its specific assignment and must remain within it.

You look to the church to serve you with the good news of redemption in Christ, to use Scripture so that as a believer you may be prepared for eternity, and to help you in this life produce fruits of faith. On the other hand, you look to the state to promote civic righteousness and to maintain law and order so that "we may live peaceful and quiet lives" (1 Timothy 2:2). You look to the state as "a judge or an arbiter" to correct wrongs that have been committed (Luke 12:14) and to serve God as "an agent of wrath to bring punishment on the wrongdoer" (Romans 13:4). To accomplish this, God has given the state "the sword" (Romans 13:4), or police power, as we call it. This includes even capital punishment.

As Christians living in this world, we are citizens of a particular state and subject to its jurisdiction. At the same time, by faith in Christ we are members of God's family, the church. As outlined above, we must distinguish between the two in our expectations of each. Unfortunately, as the Augsburg Confession notes, "some have improperly confused the power of the church with the power of the sword."[13] For this reason the confession carefully outlines the responsibility of each and the means God has given each to carry out its duties.

The church has the "power or command of God to preach the Gospel, to remit and retain sins, and to administer the sacraments."[14] Thus, "the power of the church bestows eternal things and is exercised only through the ministry of the Word."[15] But "civil government is concerned with other things than the Gospel. The state protects not souls but bodies and goods from manifest harm, and constrains men with the sword and physical penalties."[16] The following chart illustrates what is said in these quotations:

	Responsibilities	Means
Church	eternal things preach gospel forgive/retain sins administer sacraments	ministry of the Word received by faith
State	protect bodies protect goods constrain men from evil	power of the sword physical penalties earthly rewards used according to reason

To avoid confusion, neither of the two should "invade the other's functions" nor make use of the other's means.

For example, as Christian citizens we do not want the state to teach our children how to pray. The state is not to compel people to attend worship or to pay pastors' salaries nor should the state use the ministry of the Word to foster civic righteousness. On the other hand, the church is not to tell the state what laws to pass, to impose the injunctions of Scripture on the state, or to interfere with the state's power of the sword. As Christian citizens we will be concerned that our government is honest and fair and reasonable, and we will participate to make it so. But we will also remember what we can expect of each, the church and the state, and what means God has given to each.

Take the example of abortion. As a Christian, by faith I know what Scripture says about human life, that the Lord gives it at the time of conception (see Psalm 139:13-16; 51:5). I know that to destroy human life at any time is sin, and I expect my church to teach this on the basis of Scripture. However, I will not support efforts in the name of Christianity to use force (the sword) against abortion clinics. I will not expect my church, by quoting holy Scripture, to convince the government to pass laws against abortion. But as a Christian citizen, I will use every opportunity to show my fellow citizens and my government that to permit abortion is against reason and the government's responsibility to protect human life.

Thus, the church concerns itself with faith and uses the Word, and the state protects life and property with the sword on the basis of reason.

The social gospel

Some assert that the church should be the conscience of the state and a force in society, active in reforming society's ills. Advocates of what is termed the "social gospel" affirm that "the substance of the redemption of the world in Jesus Christ is adequately understood and realized only when its power is effective in the transformation of the structures of society."[17] They reduce the importance of Christ coming to redeem the sinner for eternal life in heaven. Instead, what is important is that he came to redeem society from its evils so that the world may become a better place in which to live. This changes what is expected of the church as it lives in this world because concern for reforming the individual sinner is replaced by concern for reforming society. The church's heavenly mission becomes an earthly one.

Similar is the claim that the church has a "ministry to the whole man." Some claim that in serving people for their welfare, you cannot divide between the physical and the spiritual. In fact, "holistic health requires effective functioning physically, psychologically, socially, and spiritually plus the successful integration of all these components."[18] Such a philosophy assigns responsibilities to the church that go beyond its spiritual role to the role of ministering to the "whole person." The church will practice charity by reaching out to the physical needs of people, but claiming the church is to provide ministries and services for all the needs of "the whole man" places upon it responsibilities that go beyond Scripture and sidetrack it from its saving mission and the means entrusted to it by God.

Jesus said, "My kingdom is not of this world" (John 18:36). Jesus suffered, died, and rose again so that "repentance and forgiveness of sins will be preached in his name" (Luke 24:47). Let the church remain faithful to its assigned task, to make disciples of Jesus through the means of grace. We can expect that a society will benefit from the presence of Christians, but more importantly, there is rejoicing in the presence of the angels of God as each sinner repents. And there will be eternal praises before God as the redeemed unite their heavenly voices to his glory for ever and ever.

5

The Church: Preach the gospel to whom?

"Go into all the world and preach the good news to all creation." Imagine being one of the eleven disciples who heard Jesus say this to them. "Into all the world"! "To all creation"! You might have asked: "Lord, do you mean this? Do you mean we should go beyond Judea and Galilee? Also to the Samaritans? They won't be very friendly toward us. And to Babylon, Egypt, and even Rome? And we heard of a place far beyond Rome called Spain. There are only 11 of us. The world is big. Travel is slow. What can we do?" The Lord's answer was: "You will be my witnesses in Jerusalem, and in all Judea and Samaria, and to the ends of the earth" (Acts 1:8).

Into all the world

With his Great Commission, the Lord sends the church, his believers, "into all the world." Jesus died for the sins of the world; all the world is to hear that good news. The Lord does not want "anyone to perish, but everyone to come to repentance" (2 Peter 3:9). Of the disciples we read: "Then the disciples went out and preached everywhere" (Mark 16:20). Where is "everywhere"? Where is the "world"?

Jerusalem

For the disciples, the "world" was first of all Jerusalem, and that is where they began on Pentecost day. As they continued preaching in their "hometown," "the Lord added to their number daily those who were being saved" (Acts 2:47).

For you the "world" is first of all Minneapolis or Mobridge, Los Angeles or Lake City, Oconomowoc or Oskaloosa. The "world" is where you are. To begin with, "everywhere" is your own home and family. After coming to faith in Jesus, "the first thing Andrew did was to find his brother Simon . . . And he brought him to Jesus" (John 1:41,42). Wives and husbands may hope to win over their spouses (1 Peter 3:1,2). Parents are to teach their children. That is where the "world" begins, but it doesn't end there. Your neighbors and friends, your coworkers and community are also part of "everywhere."

Judea and Samaria

For the disciples the "world" was also Judea and Samaria. When persecution broke out against the church in Jerusalem, "all except the apostles were scattered throughout Judea and Samaria . . . [and] preached the word wherever they went" (Acts 8:1,4). We may not be scattered because of persecutions, but the mobility of today's society may scatter us into many parts of our country. A job transfer may take us to Kentucky or Tennessee, to Washington or Vermont. Are we concerned about preaching the Word wherever we go?

"And Samaria." This was a territory that was hostile to the Jews. Would the Samaritans be open to a Savior who was a Jew? Philip, the evangelist, left Jerusalem and preached in Samaria, and many believed and were baptized. Hearing of this success, Peter and John also spent some time in Samaria, "preaching the gospel in many Samaritan villages" (Acts 8:25). Yes, even countries that may have been hostile to Christ and the gospel can become fertile fields for sowing the good seed of the gospel.

All the world

"To the ends of the earth." That does not seem so far anymore. The weeks it took to cross the Atlantic or Pacific are now reduced to hours. A faxed letter can reach you in minutes. Modern technology makes it possible for you to watch world events as they happen. Someone speaking in Chicago can be heard throughout the world at the time he is speaking.

That has not made the world any less hostile to the gospel, but the Lord opens doors of opportunity. As Paul preached the good news everywhere, he often suffered persecution and imprisonment. Sinful, ungodly men tried to close the doors to his preaching. But in Ephesus, Paul writes, "A great door for effective work has opened to me" (1 Corinthians 16:9). When he went to Troas, he also found that "the Lord had opened a door for me" (2 Corinthians 2:12). Even while imprisoned in Rome, he asked the Colossians to pray for him "that God may open a door for our message" (4:3). And so it is today. Sinful, ungodly men closed the doors to preaching the good news in countries dominated by communistic governments, but the omniscient and omnipotent Lord of all opens doors that men try to close. He did this in Russia when atheistic communism lost its power.

Open doors

The Lord opens doors, and the church must look for them and enter those it sees. Some of those doors are in our own United States where a church may do *home mission work*. The Lord opens other doors in the many countries of the world, and entering those is called *world mission work*. Which is the more important? Which should have priority? We can only say: The church must do the one and not neglect the other. Christians, remember the Lord's commission is to preach the gospel everywhere. This assignment was given to you, his church. He has not given it to anyone else. Unless the church proclaims the good news, it will not be heard.

Some, however, object. They say: "Why trouble people in foreign countries? They have their own cultures. They have their own religions, their own way of worshiping god. Why force your religion and culture on them?" Others say: "What these people need is not your religion but an improved economy. You must help raise their standard of living. Show them how they can develop their agriculture and their use of natural resources. Bring them the benefits of modern medicine. They don't need a message that talks about heaven; they need a social gospel that will improve their present lives."

No other way

That is not what Jesus says. He warns: "What good will it be for a man if he gains the whole world, yet forfeits his soul?" (Matthew 16:26). God has provided only one way for a soul to be saved: Believe in the Lord Jesus Christ. "There is no other name under heaven given to men by which we must be saved" (Acts 4:12). That is why the church's mission is to preach the good news in all the world. It fulfills its mission only as it leads people to repent of their sins and look in faith to Christ for forgiveness.

But what about the sick in countries where doctors and nurses are few and medical help is unavailable? What about the poverty and starvation that a drought or poor crops bring? As the church preaches the good news, it will not ignore the sick and poor, the hungry children and starving adults. It will open health centers, provide medicines, distribute food, dig wells, and do what it can to improve the lives of those who suffer. All of this, however, will not replace its gospel mission; rather, it will support the proclamation of God's mercy with acts of love and kindness. Its primary mission "to all creation" must, however, remain the Lord's command: "Preach the good news."

In the congregation

But what about those whom the Holy Spirit has already brought to faith? What responsibility does the church have toward those whom the Lord has gathered into his flock? What is the church's mission to its members? To you? To put it another way, what should Christians, who are the church, do for one another?

Nurture

You have seen pictures of starving children in Africa. For a child to live and to grow, the body needs nourishment. Loving parents want to provide what is needed. How they grieve when they see the children they gave birth to threatened by starvation!

Similarly, the Lord's Great Commission to teach and preach does not end when someone is brought to faith. Spiritual life is not to be snuffed out again because of starvation. Through teaching and preaching, the Lord wants the church to feed and nurture the new life he has created in the hearts of believers. The church has a responsibility to nurture all within its flock.

People of all ages

Included in God's flock are, first of all, the children. Parents, indeed, have primary responsibility not only for the physical but also the spiritual lives of their children. Yet, the Lord's command to his church to baptize and teach applies also to infants and children. The Lord told Peter: "Feed my lambs." Parents, be thankful that the Lord has made you part of God's family, the church. It provides various educational opportunities to help you bring up your children "in the training and instruction of the Lord" (Ephesians 6:4).

Adolescents as well as younger and older men and women are also in the congregation. In writing to Timothy and Titus, Paul instructs them how they are to serve people of all ages (1 Timothy 5:1,2; Titus 2:1-6). These all need to be nourished and nurtured spiritually while they live in a dangerous world and daily face the temptations that can destroy faith. How important are the opportunities for Bible study that the church provides in addition to regular Sunday worship!

Comfort for the troubled

The sick have a special need for the church's spiritual ministry. James writes: "Is any one of you sick? He should call the elders of the church to pray over him . . . in the name of the Lord" (5:14). Those who are sick need the visits and prayers of their brothers and sisters in the faith.

Christians will not escape the troubles of this life. They too get depressed, and the church will not ignore this. "Carry each other's burdens, and in this way you will fulfill the law of Christ" (Galatians 6:2). Paul tells the Thessalonians: "Encourage one another and build each other up, just as in fact you are doing" (1 Thessalonians 5:11). The Lord of the church reminded even the earliest New Testament Christians to nurture one another by Christian counseling.

The world, too, recognizes the importance of counseling for those who have traumatic experiences and for the troubled and depressed. Counselors are to help people cope, but all that the world can offer is counseling based on secular humanistic philosophy. This addresses itself to human reason, and hopes to build self-esteem by encouraging people to use the powers they may not even realize they have. In contrast, members of the family of God will counsel one another by pointing to the compassion and wisdom of their omnipotent heavenly Father. They will speak of his forgiving love that shows how precious we are to him. They will use the divine Word by which the Spirit of God acts powerfully in weak and troubled human hearts.

Correction for sinners

The battle against sin never ends, even for those in the family of God. Sin destroys faith, and no congregation dare ignore this. The Corinthian congregation thought it could, but Paul warns the members: "You are proud!" They did not do anything about the man guilty of incest, but Paul tells them: "Shouldn't you rather have been filled with grief and have put out of your fellowship the man who did this?" (1 Corinthians 5:2).

"You are proud!" That is true when the church ignores sin in its midst. Pride thinks that indifference toward sin will cause no harm. A proud church sets its own mind above the Word of God and fails to call sin, sin. That the world with its humanistic pride will call sex outside marriage or homosexual relationships "alternate life styles" can be expected because the world is under the rule of Satan. A church that joins the world in such claims sets itself above God's holy Word. Such arrogance will only bring harm to its members.

Therefore, the church must admonish, reprove, and correct those who fall into sin. Jesus tells us how Christians will repeatedly try to reform a sinning brother or sister (Matthew 18:15-17). Paul expresses loving concern for those who succumb to temptation when he writes: "Brothers, if someone is caught in a sin, you who are spiritual should restore him gently" (Galatians 6:1).

More than words of correction may be necessary. Paul tells the Corinthians: "Shouldn't you rather . . . have put out of your fellowship the man who did this?" The Lord Jesus told the disciples that if a sinner persists impenitently in his sin, they are to "treat him as you would a pagan or a tax collector" (Matthew 18:17). We call this excommunication.

The purpose in excluding impenitent sinners is not to give a congregation the appearance of absolute purity, as though that were possible. Even the apostle Paul in his life never reached the perfection that those demand who hold that Christians can and must become perfect or holy in their lives. In this world the church is a hospital for sinners. Likewise, the purpose of excluding impenitent sinners is not just to "get rid of all the hypocrites." Only God can look into the heart and recognize hypocrisy.

The purpose of all correction is repentance, so that "his spirit [may be] saved on the day of the Lord," as Paul tells the Corinthians (1 Corinthians 5:5). The church's mission is to sinners, to call them to repentance and assure them of the Lord's complete forgiveness in Christ for all eternity. Thus, the church will nurture God's people when they fall into sin and are in danger of eternal destruction.

A *continuing need*

Indeed, the church's mission to "preach the good news to all creation" includes you and every member of your congregation. God tells you to "let the word of Christ dwell in you richly as you teach and admonish one another with all wisdom, and as you sing psalms, hymns and spiritual songs with gratitude in your hearts to God" (Colossians 3:16).

You could see how important it is for the church to nurture its members with the saving Word when you visited Tom, whom you had not seen in church for over a year. "Don't worry about me," he assured you. "I was baptized and confirmed. My parents were good church members. I'll never give up my faith. I don't need to hear the same thing over and over again in church." You reminded him of Paul's words, "If you think you are standing firm, be careful that you don't fall!" (1 Corinthians 10:12). His response was, "I know the Ten Commandments. I'm a good husband and father. I'm not one who will fall." How much he needed to hear the same message over and over again! How much he needed to hear again and again that he is a sinner and that his sin will condemn him. How much he needed to hear again and again that he is saved alone by the grace of God in Christ, that not the good works he thinks he is doing will save him, but only the forgiveness Jesus won for him on the cross. Yes, the Christian faith needs to be nurtured, or those who once had it will turn to hopes that deceive and security that is a fiction.

Paul also recognized that those who were brought to faith needed to be nurtured. He addressed his inspired letters to people who already were Christians, to "the saints . . . , the faithful in Christ Jesus." The entire Bible is God's gift to the church so that it is equipped to meet the needs of his people.

"He who stands firm to the end will be saved" (Matthew 24:13). That is why the church needs to continually nurture and feed each Christian's faith with the Word of Life.

One mission

Some say: "The church should not spend so much time and effort preaching to itself. It is selfish to use its resources to serve those who already have heard the gospel. Its one mission is to reach out with the gospel. The Lord said, 'Go into all the world.'"

Scripture does not place the two in conflict with one another. The church does not have two missions, one to its members, another to the world. The Lord gave one command: preach and teach the good news to all creation.

That includes those who have already been brought to faith as well as the vast world of unbelievers. Both are included in the Lord's commission. You cannot do one and omit the other.

Only as the church nourishes the faith of its members with the gospel of peace will these Christians be motivated and equipped to bring the peace of the gospel to perishing sinners. Paul says of himself and his fellow Christians: "It is written: 'I believed; therefore I have spoken.' With that same spirit of faith we also believe and therefore speak" (2 Corinthians 4:13). Those who believe are moved to speak and proclaim the Word of Life to all the world.

Mission statement

The mission of the church as discussed here in chapters four and five should be recognized as the mission of every Christian congregation or church body (synod), the visible gatherings of believers through which the church functions in this world. In order to focus on its God-given mission, a congregation or synod may adopt a mission statement, which affirms the purpose of its existence. An example is the mission statement of the Wisconsin Evangelical Lutheran Synod:

> As men, women, and children united in faith and worship by the Word of God, the Wisconsin Evangelical Lutheran Synod exists to make disciples throughout the world for time and for eternity, using the gospel to win the lost for Christ and to nurture believers for lives of Christian service, all to the glory of God.[19]

6

The Church:
How does it carry out its mission?

When you joined Faith Ev. Lutheran Church of Centerville, you regularly attended the Sunday services. You considered this important, and that is why you became a member. The liturgy, the prayers and hymns, and the Scripture readings, sermon, and sacraments kept you mindful of God's mercy and love and gave you opportunity for thanksgiving and praise.

On a certain Sunday, the service folder announced the annual meeting of the congregation. One of the members invited you to come with him, and you wondered why you should attend. You were satisfied with the Sunday services. What was the purpose of this meeting? Nevertheless, you accepted the invitation.

After the opening devotion, officers of the congregation and chairmen of boards and committees presented reports. Plans were made for the next year, elections were held, and a budget was adopted. The congregation's support of missions was determined, and goals were set. You were amazed at the great amount of "business" the church had to attend to.

Objectives, goals, methods

The Lord Jesus is the head of the church. He controls, directs, and guides everything according to his wisdom and will. The Lord has placed his church into this world. As we noted earlier, his church is present in gatherings like congregations and synods, and his members live and function in this present world. His church, like every group of people living together, is subject to certain limitations and needs.

A congregation must gather for worship at a certain place. The first believers "[met] together in the temple courts" (Acts 2:46) after Pentecost day. As the church spread, believers met in houses or synagogues or alongside a river. The church needs a place or building, not because the Lord directly commands this, but to carry out its gospel mission in the world.

Like any organization or business, the church makes plans, sets objectives and goals, needs money, and provides for organization so that all things are done in an orderly way. That is the way God wants it. However, the church must never forget that it is not a mere human organization or business. It has Jesus as its head, and its objectives are determined by his Word. Human businesses and organizations have worldly objectives, which may include serving people with a good product or gaining power and prestige, but most often the final objective is to show financial profit on the bottom line. The purpose for which the church exists is to proclaim the gospel for the salvation of souls. That purpose determines its objectives, and these are rooted in Scripture. The following is an example of what a congregation or synod may include in stating its objectives:

1. To uphold and testify to the truth of God as fully revealed in the inspired, inerrant, infallible Holy Scriptures and articulated in the Lutheran Confessions;

2. To seize every opportunity the Lord provides to evangelize lost souls and establish ministering churches throughout the world;

3. To help each other grow and mature in the faith through public worship and life-long study of the Word of God;

4. To encourage and equip each other for the application of our faith in lives of Christian service, for the Lord, his church, and his world;

5. To recruit and train candidates qualified for full-time ministry and provide for their continuing education so that the Word of God is proclaimed faithfully and effectively in accord with the Lutheran Confessions.[20]

To carry out these objectives, the church needs money and property, but the acquisition of these does not become an objective of the church. The church does not exist for financial profit. As it does its work with money and property, there is no "bottom line." It receives its support from the offerings of God's people, and these offerings are a fruit of their faith, not obligations imposed by law. The church's concern is to practice good stewardship so that the offerings that God's people provide may effectively help carry out the objectives of its gospel mission.

To carry out its objectives, the church has to plan. Without planning, there is disorder, if not chaos. What the Lord told the Corinthians about their worship lives applies to all activities of the church: "Everything should be done in a fitting and orderly way" (1 Corinthians 14:40). You cannot construct a building without plans or funds. The church must plan the time of services. The pastor has to prepare his sermon and the rest of the service, and the organist must plan what to play. Joint Bible study also requires planning, and so it is with everything the congregation does, including its joint work with other congregations in the synod (mission work and training workers). Like every other human organization, the church needs to plan. All of this requires sound reasoning and good judgment in making decisions.

In its planning, however, the church will always remember: The Lord is the head of the church, and we must watch for the doors he opens. We must not think that we are in control. Paul planned to do mission work in Bithynia, but God determined otherwise (Acts 16:7-9). As in all things, so also in the church's planning we must say, "If it is the Lord's will, we will live and do this or that" (James 4:15). In planning, the church employs not only its reason, but also its faith, trusting in God's promises and leadership, and knowing that he hears the church's prayers. Reason without faith relies on man and puts him alone in control. Faith without reason may go beyond God's promises and tempt the Lord rather than hold to his Word.

Part of good planning is setting goals. Goals can help us be active in a purposeful way. They state what we want to accomplish within a determined time. The car dealer may set the goal of selling 100 cars during the month of May. Having this goal, he will determine how advertising may help him reach the goal.

The church, too, may set goals. It may determine how much money it wants to collect for a certain project, or how many missionaries it plans to send into world fields in the next year. It will then do what is necessary to reach its goals. These are matters which, to a degree at least, are within the control of the church. It can make the arrangements necessary to collect funds, and it can extend the required calls to those who are to serve as missionaries. Yet even these matters that appear to be under the church's control are still dependent on the Lord. The Holy Spirit alone can produce willing hearts that give generously, and it is the Holy Spirit who moves the missionary to accept the call he has received.

However, the church cannot set goals in some areas because they are totally outside its control. For example, the church cannot set a goal for the number of people it will bring to faith in the next year, because this is the work of the Holy Spirit. We confess: "The Holy Spirit produces faith, where and when it pleases God, in those who hear the Gospel."[21] We can set a goal for the number of preaching services we will have, when and how often we will have joint Bible study, and when and to whom to make evangelism calls, but the Holy Spirit alone works faith.

As the church plans and sets goals, and as it goes about its mission, it must not seek to become autonomous. The Lord is its head. The church goes about its work prayerfully, asking for the Lord's guidance and blessing. "Your will be done, O Lord," is part of every prayer and defines the spirit in which the church functions.

The church also follows certain methods as it pursues its goals. Paul advised the churches in Galatia and Corinth on the method they should use to collect money for the needy in Jerusalem. (Read 1 Corinthians 16:1-4.) Similarly today, weekly offering envelopes are a common method a congregation uses to gather the money required to continue its mission. A congregation may use *Robert's Rules of Order* as the method for conducting its meetings, or it may adopt a constitution that contains by-laws that may prescribe certain methods.

We must, however, remember that God does not set down any laws in Scripture that determine our methods. The church must take care lest its methods become ecclesiastical laws imposed on its members. They are nothing more than guides for orderly procedure. If they are used to motivate members toward God-pleasing action, they get in the way of the gospel. The world may use methods to motivate that appeal to pride or shame or self-esteem or that apply coercion, but the success the world may have with such methods must not tempt the church to adopt them, even if its use of such methods results in outward success. These methods are not compatible with the gospel. Only the gospel of God's love in Christ will move Christians to actions that have the Lord's approval and blessing.

Thus, because God has given no specific commands and laws in this regard, the church has freedom in setting its goals, in planning, and in adopting methods. Nevertheless, the church must remain focused on the mission God gave it and keep its objectives in mind, for these are imbedded in God's Word. Also, in every congregation, the Lord Jesus must remain the "head over everything for the church" (Ephesians 1:22). In whatever the church does, it must listen to the voice of its Redeemer and Lord as he speaks in the Scriptures.

Growth

At the conclusion of the congregational meeting, the chairman asked, "Is there any new business?" A concerned member spoke up. "I'd like to ask a question, and perhaps we should discuss it. Why doesn't our congregation grow faster? In the last five years we have grown by only 25 members. That's an average of only five per year. What's our problem?" Another member joined in, "I read of a church that grew to over 1,000 members in less than ten years. I think we should find out what they are doing and where we are failing."

The Lord wants his church to grow, both spiritually and in numbers. On the one hand, he wants the members of his family to "grow in the grace and knowledge of our Lord and Savior Jesus Christ" (2 Peter 3:18). He wants Christians who are "like newborn babies" to "grow up in your salvation." This happens as they "crave pure spiritual milk" (1 Peter 2:2). Christians are to grow spiritually and to mature in their faith.

What must the church do to bring about this growth, and what can't it do? Paul understood this well. He wrote: "I planted the seed, Apollos watered it, but God made it grow" (1 Corinthians 3:6). Any farmer or gardener will understand the point Paul is making. The seeds we plant and water will grow, but not because we have put life into them. God is the one who gives life in all of nature. The church can, and must, plant the seed of the gospel in people's hearts and water it with the water of life, but that is all it can do. It cannot reach into people's hearts and compel acceptance and growth. Spiritual life and growth is God's work and not the church's.

When the member at the meeting raised the question about the lack of his congregation's growth, he was, however, not thinking of the spiritual growth of its members. He was talking of the outward growth in numbers. In the discussion, some pointed out that they needed more members to help pay the congregation's growing expenses. Others feared that if they gained too many new members, the pleasant family feeling would be lost. Soon the members would not know one another anymore. Besides, the church building would soon become too small, and the congregation would face a very expensive building project. The pros and cons of outward growth were discussed and then referred to another meeting.

Does the Lord want his church to grow in number? There can be no question that he does. The Lord "wants all men to be saved and to come to a knowledge of the truth" (1 Timothy 2:4). The congregation in Jerusalem experienced outward growth as "the Lord added to their number daily" (Acts 2:47). The Lord has promised that his Word will be effective. As rain and snow water the earth so that it yields its fruits, so the Lord promises to make his Word "achieve the purpose for which I sent it" (Isaiah 55:11). If the church goes and makes "disciples of all nations," perceivable outward growth in numbers will follow as the Lord grants success. The Lord wants both spiritual growth in his people and outward growth in numbers.

The church, however, can become too concerned about numbers and almost obsessed with the desire for outward growth. This can become an objective in itself rather than the result of faithfully carrying out the church's scriptural purpose and objectives. Some feel the church will become a greater influence in the community because there is strength in numbers. Also, more people can help support the church financially. Growth gives the congregation a positive feeling of success. Soon, outward growth becomes a goal, and the church adopts methods that it believes cannot fail to attract more people to its fellowship. On the other hand, it is tempted to avoid doing anything that seems to stand in the way of numerical growth.

Much in Scripture does not make sense to people's natural reason. Scripture itself says that the gospel is foolishness to unbelievers. The church that is too concerned about numbers may be tempted to make God's Word and the gospel more rational, to tone down salvation "by grace alone" in favor of human cooperation, to explain miracles scientifically, to make Jesus more human than divine, to harmonize the creation account with theories that presume to describe the world's and man's origins by an evolutionary process, or to modify church practices like "close communion" that may be seen as a hindrance to growth. If the church changes biblical doctrine or practices based on Scripture, it is seeking to gain control of what God has reserved for himself. It places its own reason above revelation. If such methods are used for the sake of numerical growth, the results will be spiritual decay even if there is outward growth.

In the 1950s a missionary in India for the Disciples of Christ, Donald McGavran, was troubled by the lack of numerical growth. Certainly God wants growth. Why isn't it taking place? What can the church do to promote it? His concerns began what has become known as the Church Growth Movement.

As a movement, it is not limited to one denomination. Devotees in various churches, including some that are

Lutheran, have adopted or adapted the movement's strategies and methods. Others, however, have shown the erroneous Evangelical/Reformed theological roots of the movement and consequent unbiblical methods.[22] The movement's use of visions and goals goes beyond the church's circle of responsibility. It looks to a study and use of sociological structures to foster growth and seeks to determine which society may be most receptive to the church's message. By its emphasis on addressing the "felt needs" in a society, it shifts away from the importance of proclaiming forgiveness in Christ by a proper use of law and gospel with the ultimate goal of eternal life in heaven. "In the felt needs approach . . . sanctification becomes the means to fulfill the prospect's needs for acceptance, fulfillment, and a better life through victory over sin."[23] Let these brief examples alert us to the need to examine with discernment based on Scripture any programs and methods that have as their goal numerical growth. "Sometimes we, too, can fall into the trap of thinking that strategy spells success, and that outward success is the ultimate achievement in kingdom work."[24] Everything must be tested in the light of Scripture and the one great mission the Lord assigned to his church.

So let the church teach, teach, and continue to teach. Let it use the best preaching and teaching methods it has learned. Let it preach God's Word "in season and out of season" (2 Timothy 4:2). Let it reach out far and wide with the gospel of forgiveness in Christ. Let it plant the seed and water it. As it does this, let it remember and trust that God, according to his promise, will make the gospel grow in the hearts of the hearers. He will give both numerical and spiritual growth according to his good and gracious will.

Expectations

What kind of growth can we expect? What has God promised? What has he not promised? Are our expectations in line with God's promises?

God has promised that his Word will never fail. It will accomplish its God-appointed purpose. The gospel is called "the power of God for the salvation of everyone who believes" (Romans 1:16), so expect miracles when you speak God's Word. Turning an unbeliever to faith is indeed a miracle, and God promises such miracles. We can speak confidently when we proclaim his good news.

God has not promised that everyone who hears the good news will come to faith. The church cannot expect more success than its Lord. Jesus revealed himself as the Bread of Life whom the Father sent from heaven, as the one who came to give life to sinners. What gracious words he spoke! Yet we read: "On hearing it, many of his disciples said, 'This is a hard teaching. Who can accept it?'" (John 6:60). They turned back and no longer followed him. Jesus grieved because the people of Jerusalem rejected his loving effort to gather them as chicks under his wings (Luke 13:34). The Lord did not force his will on those who were unwilling. The Holy Spirit does not work faith with irresistible power. When Paul preached Christ and his resurrection at Athens, the result was much sneering and indifference. Only "a few men became followers of Paul and believed" (Acts 17:34). Our Savior has told us that many will enter through the wide gate that leads to destruction. Only few will find and pass through the narrow gate that leads to life (Matthew 7:13,14).

Does this make us feel that the church's mission can only hope for limited success? Will this dampen our expectations when we follow the Lord's command to "make disciples of all nations"? How do we measure success? And growth? Even one sinner who repents and turns in faith to the Lord Jesus causes rejoicing in heaven. Should the one repenting sinner bring us less joy because many failed to see their need for repentance? Dare we say that the Lord failed to provide the growth he promised? Or should we ask whether we may have failed to really communicate the good news because we relied on methods and strategies that got in the way of the gospel?

The Lord has told us that already "before the creation of the world" he chose or predestined certain people "to be adopted as his sons through Jesus Christ" (Ephesians 1:4,5). We can be assured that the Lord will bring all his elect to faith and salvation. When Paul preached in Antioch, "all who were appointed for eternal life believed" (Acts 13:48). Not one of God's elect will be unreached, for "those he predestined, he also called" (Romans 8:30). Not one of the elect will lose salvation. Even the "false Christs and false prophets" with their "signs and miracles" will not be able "to deceive the elect." Yet for their sake the Lord will shorten those final days (Mark 13:20-22). These are God's promises.

Will these promises of God lead to a fatalistic attitude toward mission outreach? Will they lead Christians to say: "The Lord will save his elect. Nothing I do will bring this about or prevent this. The Lord doesn't need me"? Human reason may ask such questions, but faith remembers all the promises and commands of God. It does not question God when our reason does not comprehend all of God's inscrutable ways. Instead, it relies on what God has revealed for our comfort, encouragement, and guidance: Christ Jesus died for the sins of the whole world; God wants all people to be saved through faith in Christ; he commanded us to go and preach this good news in all the world; and through this preaching God has determined to gather those whom he chose before the creation of the world for salvation. We will not ask: Why did he choose some and not others? Is this person to whom I am speaking one of God's elect? Why doesn't God simply work faith in the hearts of all people? The Christian will not permit his reason to ask questions the Lord has not answered in Scripture. In faith the church and its members will strive to carry out the gospel mission the Lord has given them. The church will reach out confidently, knowing that the Lord will surely bring his elect into his fold through its preaching and teaching.

Conclusion to Part II

"The church should not spend so much time preaching about eternal life. It should concern itself with our present life." "Our congregation is sending too much money to world missions. We should keep it in the congregation to help pay for the new fellowship hall." "Our Christian day school costs too much. The church shouldn't be in the business of education." "I don't know why the pastor is after me to come to Bible class. I learned all I need when I was confirmed." Not all people agree on what the church's mission is and how it is to carry out its work.

In thinking about these things, you must begin with questions like these: Why are you a member of the church? What do you expect of it? What is its mission? And yours? The Lord Jesus gives the answer in the Great Commission: "Go and make disciples of all nations." "Preach the good news to all creation." What a simple and yet stupendous mission!

It is difficult for the church to stick to its task, and the history of Roman Catholicism shows how tempting it is for the church to become a power in the world. Many Protestant and Reformed churches have turned from saving people for eternity to saving society from its present ills. When the gospel seems slow in producing results, we are tempted to help it along with methods and skills of our devising. We think human persuasion must help where the Spirit is being resisted and that logical explanations must make God's mysteries and miracles rationally acceptable.

We seem to be few in number among the world's billions. In each generation, compared to the multitudes of unbelievers, "few" enter eternal life at the narrow gate. But as they hear the Lord's gracious welcome, "Come, you who are blessed by my Father; take your inheritance, the kingdom prepared for you since the creation of the world" (Matthew 25:34), they will join the redeemed of all times and places. What a host that will be, a multitude too great to count, "from every nation, tribe, people and language, standing before the throne and in front of the Lamb." Wearing white robes and holding palm branches in their hands, they will fill heaven with their loud voices as they cry: "Salvation belongs to our God, who sits on the throne, and to the Lamb" (Revelation 7:9,10). This is the ultimate objective of the church's mission: Glory to God in the highest!

Part III

The Ministry of the Church

7

The Ministry: Who is a minister?

"Last Sunday we had a guest preacher. He encouraged our young people to study for the ministry. He said we needed many more pastors and teachers." "Several Sundays ago our pastor said in a sermon that we are all ministers. The way he explained it made sense, but now I'm confused. Who is a minister?"

Ministry is service

"Whosoever will be great among you, let him be your minister" (Matthew 20:26 KJV). In the NIV this verse is translated: "Whoever wants to become great among you must be your servant." The Greek word that the KJV translated "minister" is translated "servant" in the NIV. A minister is a servant, and ministry is service.

When Jesus spoke these words he was not telling his disciples that someone becomes great by becoming a minister in the sense of a pastor. Rather, by serving people one becomes great. He points to himself: "Just as the Son of Man did not come to be served, but to serve, and to give his life as a ransom for many" (Matthew 20:28). Thus, every pastor is a minister or servant, but not every minister or servant is a pastor. So the question arises: Who in the church is a minister or servant?

Service has two aspects. A servant serves the one who gives the commands. He also serves those who benefit from his service. Even Jesus said of himself that he was sent to do the Father's will, but at the same time he served the whole world of sinners by becoming the ransom for their sins. When we speak of ministers or servants in the church, who are they? And whose servants are they? Whom do they serve? What service is expected of them?

Ministry of the gospel

In the previous part we considered the church's mission. When our Savior gave his church its great commission, he also designated those who were to serve in carrying it out. To whom was Jesus speaking when he said, "Go and make disciples"? Or when he commanded, "Preach the good news"? He was talking to his disciples, those who believed in him. That includes not only the Twelve, but all who until the "end of the age" would come to faith. That includes you and me.

To whom were they to go? Whom are they, or we, to serve? "All creation." This includes people everywhere in the whole world. What is the assignment? They, and we, are to communicate the good news of salvation, the gospel. Through the ministry of the gospel, the Holy Spirit brings people to faith and keeps them in the faith. "Faith comes from hearing the message, and the message is heard through the word of Christ" (Romans 10:17). We acknowledge this in the Augsburg Confession: "In order that we may obtain this faith, the ministry of teaching the Gospel and administering the sacraments was instituted."[25]

Ministry of the keys

Sometimes we speak of the ministry of the gospel as the ministry of the keys. Peter, speaking for all the disciples, had made a good confession to Jesus, calling him "the Christ, the Son of the living God." Jesus told Peter, "I will give you the keys of the kingdom of heaven; whatever you bind on earth will be bound in heaven, and whatever you loose on earth will be loosed in heaven" (Matthew 16:19).

On the basis of this passage the Roman pope claims special power in the church for himself. He maintains that since Jesus gave Peter the keys, he alone has the power of binding and loosing, of opening or closing heaven through the power of excommunication. What is more, the pope, claiming to be Peter's successor, says he has exclusive use of the keys today. The pope has used this power quite arbitrarily to force his will on people. It was unsuccessfully used against Luther to force him to recant his teachings.

Is it true that Jesus gave the keys of the kingdom of heaven only to Peter? In Matthew 18:18, we hear Jesus giving the same binding and loosing power to all the disciples. The Roman pope's conclusion is false. Likewise, his claim to be Peter's successor is false.

What is the binding and loosing Jesus speaks about? In John 20:23 Jesus states it in these words: "If you forgive anyone his sins, they are forgiven; if you do not forgive them, they are not forgiven." Loosing is forgiving sins;

binding is not forgiving sins. Jesus again was speaking to all the disciples, including you and all believers. God has entrusted his keys to Christians, individually and collectively.

How can you forgive sins? There is only one way. You say to the penitent sinner: "For the sake of Jesus' death, your sins are forgiven." The gospel is the key that looses sins, that opens heaven. To the individual penitent sinner, it applies the forgiveness which Jesus won on the cross for the whole world. Faith lays hold of that forgiveness, trusting that Jesus' word is true.

This loosing key was used by the prophet Nathan. David confessed his sin of adultery and murder: "I have sinned against the LORD." To penitent David, Nathan could say: "The LORD has taken away your sin" (2 Samuel 12:13). John sums this up for us in these words: "If we confess our sins, he is faithful and just and will forgive us our sins" (1 John 1:9). The church, which includes all believers, must speak this word of forgiveness, using the loosing key.

This same gospel, when it is withheld, "retains sins" and closes heaven. Those who deny their sins, delight in them, feel no remorse over them, and want to continue in them are impenitent. John writes: "If we claim to be without sin, we deceive ourselves and the truth is not in us" (1 John 1:8). Until someone repents, the gospel of forgiveness must be withheld. That is the binding key. The full condemnation of the law still rests on this person because of impenitence or unbelief. "Whoever does not believe will be condemned" (Mark 16:16).

Jesus tells the individual Christian what to do "if your brother sins against you." "Show him his fault, just between the two of you" (Matthew 18:15ff.). Calling a sinner to repentance is the personal responsibility of every Christian, and if the sinner repents, you will tell him he is forgiven. If he does not listen to you as an individual, "take one or two others along." But what if these efforts also fail? Do not give up. Jesus says further: "Tell it to the church." Perhaps this larger gathering of Christians will convince him of his sin and bring him to a contrite confession; you are still hoping to apply the loosing key. However, "if he refuses to listen even to the church, treat him as you would a pagan or a tax collector." He is excluded from the congregation when the binding key is applied, and "whatever you bind on earth will be bound in heaven."

In the Small Catechism, Luther describes the use of the keys for binding and loosing as follows:

> A Christian congregation with its called pastor uses the keys in accordance with Christ's command, by forgiving those who repent of their sin and are willing to amend, and by excluding from the congregation those who are plainly impenitent that they may repent. . . . when this is done, it is as valid and certain in heaven also, as if Christ, our dear Lord, dealt with us himself.

Priesthood of all believers

When the pastor said that every Christian is a minister, or servant, he was referring to what is generally called the priesthood of all believers. To appreciate what this means let's take a look into the Old Testament.

Among God's people in the Old Testament times, only the descendants of Aaron could serve as priests. Their specific responsibility was to serve in the temple and bring the various sacrifices that God required. That is the way these priests served God and his people. All of that came to an end when Jesus, our high priest, offered himself as the one perfect sacrifice. "We have been made holy through the sacrifice of the body of Jesus Christ once for all" (Hebrews 10:10). It was impossible for the former sacrifices, which consisted in "the blood of bulls and goats" to take away sins. That is why they had to be repeated as a "reminder of sins." These sacrifices performed according to God's law were "only a shadow of the good things that are coming—not the realities themselves" (Hebrews 10:1,3). In Christ the reality of complete forgiveness once for all is here. The sacrifices that were shadows have ended, and so has the special order of priests that performed them for the people.

Now in the New Testament, Peter refers to all believers as "a chosen people, a royal priesthood, a holy nation, a people belonging to God" (1 Peter 2:9). Believers belong to God in a very special way. He has chosen them to be his very own, and he paid the price of his Son's blood to redeem them from sin. That blood cleansed them so that God declares them holy. He calls his people a "royal priesthood" or, as in verse five, "a holy priesthood." Think of it! When the Lord brought you to faith and made you his own, he said to you, "You now are one of my priests."

You, of course, are not to function by offering the Old Testament sacrifices. Those shadows are a thing of the past, and you certainly are not to bring some kind of further sacrifice for sin. "There is no longer any sacrifice for sin" (Hebrews 10:18). Jesus accomplished this *once for all*. Free from sin, you now belong to a "holy priesthood" that offers "spiritual sacrifices acceptable to God through Jesus Christ" (1 Peter 2:5). Let's look at some of these spiritual sacrifices that please God because they are brought through faith in the Lord Jesus.

God made you his priest so that "you may declare the praises of him who called you out of darkness into his wonderful light" (1 Peter 2:9). You are to praise and glorify God by telling people how Jesus brought light into your sin-darkened heart. As you personally lead another sinner out of darkness to the light of the gospel, you are bringing a spiritual sacrifice precious to your God. The Lord gave you the gospel and made you one of his priests so that you might pass the good news on to others. Nothing brings God greater glory and praise than for you to say, "Take my lips and let them be filled with messages from thee" (*Christian Worship* [CW] 469:3).

Your prayers are also spiritual sacrifices you offer to God. The Lord wants you as a priest to come with your petitions, praises, and thanksgiving. Pray not only for yourself since the Lord invites us also to "pray for each other" (James 5:16). He wants you to call on him "in the day of trouble," your trouble or that of anyone else. What glory comes to him as he keeps his promises of deliverance! What glory is his when we then honor him with our spiritual sacrifice of thanksgiving (Psalm 50:14,15)!

Turning a fellow Christian from sin is another type of spiritual sacrifice. "If someone is caught in a sin, you who are spiritual should restore him gently" (Galatians 6:1). Or "if one of you should wander from the truth and someone should bring him back, remember this: Whoever turns a sinner from the error of his way will save him from death" (James 5:19,20). The Lord is honored by such spiritual sacrifices on the part of his "priests."

"Take my life and let it be consecrated, Lord, to thee. Take my moments and my days; let them flow in ceaseless praise" (CW 469:1). Paul urges Christians "to offer your bodies as living sacrifices, holy and pleasing to God—this is your spiritual act of worship" (Romans 12:1). When people see you live your life as a Christian, when they see that you serve God through a life in service to others and not of self, when you let your light shine, when your Christianity shows in what you say and do, this brings glory to your Father in heaven (Matthew 5:16). Your spiritual sacrifice is to say, "Take myself, and I will be ever, only, all for thee" (CW 469:6).

"Everyone a minister"

"In Christ we who are many form one body." That is the church. Paul goes on to say about every believer, "Each member belongs to all the others" (Romans 12:5). If we belong to one another, we will serve or minister to one another because every member is a servant or minister.

With this in mind, the Lord gave gifts to each of his members. They are not all the same. Paul mentions some of these different gifts: prophesying, serving, teaching, encouraging, contributing to the needs of others, leading others, and showing mercy (Romans 12:6-8). Each gift may lend itself to serving in a different way, even as an eye does not serve the same purpose in the human body as the ear or tongue or foot. We must remember, however, that they are all gifts of the Spirit, given by God "for the common good."

As one of God's elect priests, you will want to use the gifts God has given to you in your personal life and in the many contacts you have with other people. You will let your light shine, as the Lord gives opportunity. As a parent or child, brother or sister, relative or friend, or fellow worker or neighbor, you will remember that you are one of God's royal priests. You will function in a way that your gifts may serve others in their needs.

The mission of the church is also your life's mission. Yes, "everyone is a minister," everyone whom the Lord has made one of his royal priests. Your lips have a message, the good news of salvation. Your life has a purpose, to "declare the praises of him who called you out of darkness into his wonderful light" (1 Peter 2:9). You, and every individual Christian, have an important *personal ministry.*

But what about your pastor? Have you replaced him? Since everyone is a minister, is there no need for a pastor? The fact that the Lord made every Christian a priest who is to serve or minister does not make every believer a pastor. The Lord has more to say about this. The next chapter will concern itself with the *public ministry.*

8

The Ministry: What is the public ministry?

Your congregation held a special meeting to call a pastor. The pastor who had served your congregation for the past 20 years had retired. You were not sure how you should go about calling a replacement. For the first time in 20 years, your congregation was looking for someone to serve you in the public ministry. Many questions were discussed. What are a pastor's responsibilities? What will you expect of him? How do you find out who is qualified? You even wondered whether your congregation's needs required special qualifications. How should the actual calling be done? What about the salary and other benefits? Calling a new pastor gave your congregation the opportunity to discuss the whole subject of the public ministry. You were thankful that you could turn to your synod for help. You appreciated that a representative of your synod was present as your advisor.

The public ministry

Ministry is service. The *public* ministry, then, is public service. *Public* may mean the opposite of *private*. When something is done as a public service, that may mean that it takes place in the presence of many people, out in the open where others can observe what is happening. The action is not done in private. More, however, is involved when we speak of a person holding a public *office*. A public official, a senator or governor or policeman, acts not simply as an individual person, but on behalf of and for the benefit of those who have placed him or her into office.

Similarly, whoever serves the church in the public ministry is not functioning as an individual person, but for those who have called him. Such a person does much work in public. For example, when the pastor preaches, he does not do so in private, but out in the open for all to hear. When, however, he gives communion to someone in the hospital, he does so in private, and we call it "private communion." When he counsels someone, he does so confidentially in a private setting. But, whether the pastor serves before many people or in a private situation, he is serving in the public ministry. In either case he is doing something required of him as the congregation's pastor. Since he is serving on behalf of the congregation, such public ministry is sometimes also called *representative ministry*, in contrast to an individual Christian's personal ministry.

Instituted by God

At the meeting at which your congregation intended to call a pastor, the synodical advisor explained that you were not just hiring a worker for your congregation. He pointed out that you were asking the Lord to give you a pastor. In fact, those who serve in the public ministry are serving because the Lord has given them to the congregation for this service. This sounded strange because you were going to choose the person by a ballot vote, just as you did when you hired the contractor to build your church. Was something different happening here? Was this an idea your synod was promoting to enhance the position of the pastor? Or was this something that God himself teaches in the Bible?

It is important to know that God himself instituted the public ministry for his church. It is important to acknowledge that the Lord Jesus gives the church its public servants. From among his disciples, Jesus "appointed twelve—designating them apostles—that they might be with him and that he might send them out to preach" (Mark 3:14). What distinguished the apostles from the other disciples is that they were chosen for special training and then sent out to preach. They became the first to serve in the public ministry of the New Testament church. They preached on Pentecost day and served as the first pastors of the Jerusalem congregation.

Even after his ascension, the Lord Jesus continues to give his church the servants it needs. The one who "ascended higher than all the heavens . . . gave some to be apostles, some to be prophets, some to be evangelists, and some to be pastors and teachers" (Ephesians 4:10,11). The apostles whom Jesus gave to the early church were unique because the Holy Spirit used them to give the church the inspired Scriptures of the New Testament. The Lord has not promised his church further "apostles" through whom he will give the church further inspired writings. Rather, the church is to judge all future writing and teaching by means of the inspired writings of the prophets, apostles, and evangelists as we have them in the Bible. However, the Lord does continue to give the church those who may be sent out to preach (apostles in that sense) and who will serve the church with the Word, such as prophets, evangelists, pastors, and teachers. They do not all function in the same way, but they all are in the public ministry of the Word which the Lord instituted. Scripture also uses other titles for them, like bishop, overseer, presbyter, elder, shepherd, and deacon. All these are given by the Lord to serve his church in the public ministry.

The Lord gives them to his church so that the gospel may be preached in an orderly way. We heard that all Christians are to "preach the good news to all creation," but consider what could happen in a congregation of Christians, who all are part of the "universal priesthood," with the command to "preach." Scripture reports what happened in Corinth; public worship became disorderly. Too many people wanted to use their particular spiritual gifts before the assembled congregation. Paul reminded them that "God is not a God of disorder but of peace" (1 Corinthians 14:33) and advised that two or three should speak, one after the other. The others can listen and carefully weigh what is said. Through the Word they hear, they will be built up in their faith. For the spiritual well-being of the entire congregation, public preaching was to be done in an orderly manner. To this end, God instituted the public ministry and gives the church those who serve in this manner. "Everything should be done in a fitting and orderly way" (v. 40).

Different forms of the public ministry

Just as the most common grouping of Christians is the local congregation, so also the most common form of the public ministry is that of the pastor of a congregation. God wants every congregation to be provided with the Word and sacraments. The congregation expects the pastor to serve them by preaching and by administering Baptism and the Lord's Supper. The members look to him to counsel them, to instruct and confirm their children, to conduct Bible classes, to visit the sick, to comfort the dying, and to conduct Christian funeral services. The entire congregational organization, with its committees and boards, as well as the ladies', men's, and youth groups are usually under his supervision. Surely in the church today, the most comprehensive and common form of the public ministry is that of the congregation's pastor.

But what shall a congregation do when its pastor cannot perform all these many functions alone? The congregation at Jerusalem gives us the answer. Even the 12 apostles who were serving them could not take care of all the work, which included distributing food to the widows of the congregation. There were complaints. By attempting to do everything themselves, the apostles were in danger of neglecting the ministry of the Word, but that would not be right. Their solution was this: "Brothers, choose seven men from among you who are known to be full of the Spirit and wisdom. We will turn this responsibility [of serving the widows] over to them" (Acts 6:3). Thus the needs within the congregation led them to establish another form of the public ministry in their midst, that of looking after the congregation's works of charity. The men who were chosen are often referred to as deacons.

Was this proper? Did the Lord directly command them to do this? We answer "Yes" to the first question and "No" to the second. The Lord blessed what they had done for we read: "So the word of God spread. The number of disciples in Jerusalem increased rapidly" (Acts 6:7). Yet the Lord had not led them to this solution by any specific command. The congregation was free to solve the "public ministry" problem according to circumstances, using its best judgment.

We already noted that the ascended Lord gave his church some to serve as apostles, as prophets, as evangelists, as pastors and teachers (Ephesians 4:11). Scripture does not give us an exact job description for each of these ministries, and nowhere does the Lord command us to have those same offices in the church today. It is doubtful that our present position of pastor corresponds completely to any one of them. Scripture leads us to the conclusion: "The one public ministry of the Gospel may assume various forms, as circumstances demand."[26]

Thus, the Lord gives his church today some as pastors and teachers, others as professors, as synod and district officers, as world missionaries, as administrators, as stewardship counselors, etc. Scripture gives no specific word of institution for any of these forms. All of them, however, are forms of the divinely mandated public ministry of the gospel. They all contribute to the public proclamation of the Word so that the church may be edified.

Some assert that only one office was instituted by the Lord himself, that of pastor of a local congregation, and that all other forms of the public ministry are auxiliary offices and are of human origin.[27] We must say in response to this that there is no word of institution for the pastorate of a local congregation or of any particular form of the public ministry. No laws in the New Testament command the exact form of the pastorate. In the Old Testament God had done this through ceremonial laws that applied to the high priest, the priests, and the Levites. They were commanded what to wear, what to eat, what sacrifices to bring, and what festivals to observe. All details of their temple service were established by law, and there were severe penalties for disobedience.

All of this ended with the coming of Christ, who fulfilled what those laws foreshadowed. "Therefore do not let anyone judge you by what you eat or drink, or with regard to a religious festival, a New Moon celebration or a Sabbath day" (Colossians 2:16). God did not replace the laws that had been set aside with new ceremonial laws that were to apply to the New Testament church and its ministry. Hence, all ceremonial forms, including the forms the public ministry may assume, are now a matter of Christian liberty.

The Roman Catholic Church fails to recognize this freedom. Rome has set up a hierarchical ministerial structure by ceremonial laws of its own making. It claims that the pope, as the successor of Peter, is the supreme head of the church. The bishops, by a process called the "apostolic succession," are the successors of the apostles. As in the Old Testament, priests form a class distinct from the laity. Rome claims this clerical hierarchy is an institution of God that must function according to specific ecclesiastical laws. These teachings and practices of Rome remind us of the Old Testament with its ceremonial laws. They conflict with the New Testament public ministry of the Word established by God, a ministry that has no laws that dictate its structure and form.

Motivated by the gospel, the church is indeed intent on following the Lord's will regarding his gospel. Besides telling every Christian to be a preacher of the gospel, the Lord has established the public ministry of the Word. Following the Lord's will for good order, a congregation of Christians will set up its public ministry of the gospel according to whatever forms will best serve the welfare of his church and glorify God, the Lord of all.

9

The Ministry:
What is the call into the public ministry?

When the representative from your synod helped your congregation find a new pastor, he stressed that calling a pastor was not the same as choosing and hiring someone to paint the inside of your church building. You wondered about this. In what way was it different? As he explained the entire calling process, the difference became evident.

The need for a call

Just what is a call? The Bible says that Christians have been "called to be saints" (Romans 1:7). Paul tells the Thessalonian Christians that God "called you to this [saving faith] through our gospel" (2 Thessalonians 2:14). God chose us, and through the gospel he made us what we are as Christians. We can say that every Christian has a call from God to be what he is, a member of God's family and a witness for Christ. We already took note of the fact that every Christian has been called to a personal ministry.

But how does an individual Christian enter the public ministry? The Bible also speaks of certain individuals being called into special public service. The author of Hebrews writes about Aaron and the high priests who served in the temple: "No one takes this honor upon himself; he must be called by God, just as Aaron was" (Hebrews 5:4). When God called someone, whether to be a priest or prophet, he chose that person and placed him into his position of public service. This was another call in addition to the call to be an individual Christian.

We see that in either case God is the one who is active in a call. He is the one who calls a sinner to become one of his children, and he is the one who calls one of his believers to serve in the public ministry. In either case God places someone into a particular position. God does not hire us to serve him on the basis of an agreement we make with him. It is not by means of some agreed upon deal that we become Christians. It is also not by some agreed upon contract that someone serves in the public ministry. God's call is a one-way action.

What is more, unless God calls us, we cannot serve. To the "wicked," or unbelievers, God says: "What right have you to recite my laws or take my covenant on your lips?" (Psalm 50:16). Only Christians are called to be his witnesses. Similarly, a special call is necessary to serve in the public ministry. Paul asks the question: "How can they preach unless they are sent?" (Romans 10:15). Someone must send or call those who are to serve in the public preaching ministry. Thus, in the Augsburg Confession we affirm "that nobody should publicly teach or preach or administer the sacraments in the church without a regular call."[28]

A regular call

What is a "regular call" into the public ministry? We can ask this question in another way. How does God give the church its public servants? We know that the apostles were chosen directly by the Lord Jesus. He also directly chose Saul, or Paul, to be his apostle. In writing to the Galatians, Paul stresses that he is an apostle "sent not from men nor by man, but by Jesus Christ and God the Father" (1:1). Paul, like the other apostles and like Moses and Isaiah and others in the Old Testament, was called by the Lord in a direct, personal manner. We speak of this as a direct or immediate call from God.

But the Lord Jesus is no longer visibly present on earth. He does not directly speak to someone and call him to be the pastor of a certain congregation. He also has not promised to appear before a congregation in some special way and directly tell it who is to be its pastor. But he does promise, "where two or three come together in my name, there am I with them" (Matthew 18:20). So he is with the Christian congregation as it assembles in his name to choose, or call, a fellow Christian to be its pastor. Through the call of such a group of Christians, to whom God has entrusted his Word, the Lord gives his church its public servants. Most often this group of Christians is the voters' assembly of a local congregation. It may also be a board or commission calling in behalf of a church body, or it may be the board of a Lutheran high school or institutional mission.

The pope in Rome claims that only he, through his bishops, can ordain priests or pastors. A congregation must receive them from him. Episcopalians insist that a congregation receives its pastors through the bishops, who are the successors of the apostles. It is rather the congregation, made up of God's chosen people, that calls someone to serve it in the public ministry. The synodical representative is only an advisor, but he can guide the congregation to choose someone who is properly qualified. Only at the request of the congregation may someone make the choice for them. This is done, for example, when a seminary graduate is called to a congregation. The choice of the person is left up to the synod's assignment committee. It is, however, still the congregation calling.

Is such a call "from men [or] by man," as Paul puts it in Galatians 1:1, truly a call from the Lord? Or are only human beings, fellow Christians, calling? Speaking to the elders of Ephesus, who had no direct call like the apostles, Paul says that "the Holy Spirit has made you overseers" over the flock in Ephesus (Acts 20:28). The Holy Spirit calls through the church when it calls, and that is a "regular call."

Luther stressed the importance of the congregation's call into the public ministry. He writes: "Because we are all priests of equal standing, no one must push himself forward and take it upon himself, without our consent and election, to do that for which we all have equal authority. For no one dare take upon himself what is common to all without the authority and consent of the community."[29] Against those who claimed to have a direct call from the Holy Spirit, Luther wrote: "Today He [God] calls all of us into the ministry of the Word by a mediated call, that is, one that comes through means, namely, through man. . . . Nevertheless, it is divine. . . . Since the time of the apostles this has been the usual method of calling in the world. It should not be changed; it should be exalted, on account of the sectarians, who despise it and lay claim to another calling, by which they say that the Spirit drives them to teach."[30]

Among today's "sectarians," as Luther refers to them, are those bodies that are influenced by the Pentecostal view that the Holy Spirit works directly in the human heart, apart from Word and sacraments. So also they claim that the Holy Spirit directly calls them to public ministry. The Holy Spirit indeed, through the means of grace, may move an individual Christian to set "his heart on being an overseer [pastor]" (1 Timothy 3:1). That, however, is not a call to active service in the public ministry, but this moves an individual to prepare and become available for a call through the church.

How should a congregation or group of Christians go about calling someone into the public ministry? God does not give his church a set of laws defining the calling process. Paul left Titus in Crete so that he might "appoint elders in every town" (Titus 1:5). We are not told exactly how Titus did this. It is doubtful that he appointed the elders without participation from the congregations. We have a somewhat more complete description of the procedure used when the Jerusalem church chose the seven deacons: they described the position that would take care of the need they had; they took note of the required qualifications; and they chose seven people with those qualifications (Acts 6:1-6). Scripture does not inform us whether they had a larger list of qualified candidates and chose the seven by ballot or raising of hands, or whether they nominated and voted on each in turn, or whether they used some other method of choosing.

Methods are a matter of Christian liberty. The calling church generally follows a procedure similar to that used in Jerusalem: determine the needs, adopt a list of qualified candidates, and complete the election by majority vote. The congregation agrees to make the election its unanimous choice. This may appear to differ little from the methods any group may use to decide whom to hire for a certain job, but the church will remember that the Lord is involved in what it is doing. He is the one who calls. The church is the body through whom the Lord calls. The members will pray that the Lord be with them and bless them, and they will ask the Holy Spirit to guide them in all they do. With such a prayer in their hearts and on their lips, they will act in the fear of God, using their best judgment in accordance with the Lord's will as revealed in the Scriptures.

Qualifications for the public ministry

As you met with the representative of your synod to call a pastor, the question came up: "What are we looking for in our new pastor?" The father of several teenagers spoke up, "We need someone who is good with young people." Another replied, "We need someone who is outgoing and friendly and good with people of all ages. Our former pastor was more inclined to spend time at his desk. I know he prepared good sermons, but I hope our new pastor will get out more among the people." "We're in an expanding community," a third agreed, "and it's important that he's good at evangelism."

The congregation may recognize qualifications that will be helpful for its particular situation. But what is the will of the Lord, who instituted the public ministry? What qualifications does he tell the church to look for?

We listen to God as he speaks in 1 Timothy 3:1-7 and Titus 1:6-9.

As to his person, he is to be "above reproach" and "blameless." This does not speak of being blameless in the sight of God. Before God we all are guilty sinners. It is only through faith in the finished redemption Jesus effected on Calvary's cross that God declares us to be saints. *Blameless* has reference to the pastor's life and conduct. In the eyes of his fellow Christians, a pastor must be "above reproach," and he must "have a good reputation with outsiders." Though all Christians should strive for this qualification, it should be present to an even greater degree in the lives of those the church calls as its public servants. Some specific areas in which the pastor is to be above reproach are mentioned by Paul.

"The husband of but one wife" points to being above reproach in his sexual life. Those who repent of fornication and adultery are forgiven and continue as members of God's family. They are, however, no longer "blameless" as a qualification for public service.

"Not given to drunkenness" eliminates anyone who cannot control his use of intoxicating beverages or other drugs that are destructive of body and mind.

"Not a lover of money." The greedy pastor serves another master besides the Lord. He may succumb to the temptation of "pursuing dishonest gain."

"Temperate, self-controlled, respectable, hospitable" are some positive characteristics that contribute to being blameless in his person.

Among the qualifications that Paul lists are skills the pastor, or public servant, needs because of the nature of his assignment. These may be natural abilities he possesses or skills he has acquired through training and experience.

Basic is "able to teach," and that includes being able to learn. Paul instructs Timothy: "The things you have heard me say in the presence of many witnesses entrust to reliable men who will also be qualified to teach others" (2 Timothy 2:2). God tells the church to educate those it intends to call. The people it trains are to be "reliable," which includes having the ability to learn and apply what is learned. The goal of the training is to make them capable, reliable preachers and teachers, or communicators. Of prime importance is the subject matter: the gospel, or the divine Word of Truth God spoke through Paul and the other inspired writers. Being reliable also means that "he must hold firmly to the trustworthy message as it has been taught." That will enable the pastor to "encourage others by sound doctrine and refute those who oppose it" (Titus 1:9). Thus, ministerial education must have a high priority in a church body's program and budget. Then its congregations can be assured of pastors and teachers who are "able to teach" as God would have it done.

Managerial skill is another of the pastor's qualifications. This involves working with people, helping them function together in an orderly and peaceful manner. What may reveal the presence or absence of this skill? Paul wrote to Timothy: "He must manage his own family well and see that his children obey him with proper respect. (If anyone does not know how to manage his own family, how can he take care of God's church?)" (1 Timothy 3:4,5). He must be "a man whose children believe and are not open to the charge of being wild and disobedient" (Titus 1:6).

Paul mentions further qualifications that may also contribute toward being an able teacher and administrator: "not violent but gentle, not quarrelsome" (1 Timothy 3:3), "self-controlled, upright, holy and disciplined" (Titus 1:8).

During the calling process, a congregation will listen carefully as the Lord speaks of the qualifications he looks for in a public minister. Not everyone will have these in equal measure. The congregation may determine which are of special importance in its situation. In any case, "hold[ing] firmly to the trustworthy message" and the "ability to teach" must have the highest priority.

How and where will a congregation find someone with the necessary qualifications? It will appreciate the help of the synodical advisor, who will propose people who are properly trained and have the needed qualifications.

At the call meeting, one of the members raised further questions. "For how long a term are we calling the new pastor? Wouldn't it be advisable to try him out for a year? If we like him, we can extend the call for a longer time." However, the congregation was not just hiring someone to do a job to their liking; through the congregation the Lord is calling someone to serve according to his liking. If the pastor were called for a year, he would be tempted to try to be popular so he would be reelected. He might become a servant of men rather than of God (see Galatians 1:10). Since a vicar is available for only one year, he receives a one-year call. A vacancy pastor is called for only the duration of the vacancy. A permanent pastor should receive a permanent call, that is, one without a fixed time of service.

Duties and accountability

A list of duties outlining the responsibilities of everyone who is called into the public ministry does not exist. Even Paul was not called to do everything that may be included in a pastor's or missionary's call. He says, "Christ did not send me to baptize" (1 Corinthians 1:17). The duties of those who serve will differ according to the needs of a congregation. Not all pastors have the same duties in every congregation, especially when there is more than one pastor in the congregation. The calling body will state in each case what is expected in the type of ministry to which it calls.

In assigning duties, a congregation will not ask a woman to assume duties that require her to serve in a way that is not in agreement with her created role as a "helper" (Genesis 2:7,18,22). A congregation will not call her to a position where she would "have authority over a man" (1Timothy 2:12), where she would not "be in submission, as the Law says" (1 Corinthians 14:34). The primary example of this would be to ask her to serve as pastor of a congregation. On the other hand, the church is pleased to have her serve in positions for which she may be especially qualified, such as that of teaching children, or counseling teenagers, mothers, wives, or widows.[31]

The calling congregation or group also has responsibilities. Paul reminds the Corinthians that "men ought to regard us as servants of Christ" (1 Corinthians 4:1). The called servants are not just hired help. Thus, "the elders who direct the affairs of the church well are worthy of double honor, especially those whose work is preaching and teaching" (1 Timothy 5:17). This is not simply to honor a called servant personally for work well done, but it is to glorify and praise the Lord whom he serves.

God also expects that "those who preach the gospel should receive their living from the gospel" (1 Corinthians 9:14). Paul uses the example of the plowman and thresher who do their work in the hope of sharing in the harvest. "If we have sown spiritual seed among you, is it too much if we reap a material harvest from you?" (1 Corinthians 9:11). The spiritual seed, the gospel in Word and sacraments, however, is always a free gift from God. Nothing material, the salary and benefits paid to the pastor, can purchase these blessings or serve as a repayment for them. Luther writes: "Because this stupendous and incalculable gift cannot be administered except by men who need food and clothing, it is necessary to nourish and support them. This, however, is not payment for the gift; it is payment for the service and the work."[32] In this way a congregation may show "double honor" toward those who serve it with the Lord's priceless spiritual blessings.

Since the congregation assigns its pastor's duties and pays his salary, the question may arise: To whom is he accountable? The painter whom the congregation hires is accountable to the congregation for his work. What about those in the public ministry? They are "servants of Christ." As such, Paul says, "It is the Lord who judges me" (1 Corinthians 4:4). The pastor you call to your congregation is accountable primarily to the Lord. To forget this is to forget that the Lord called him. To forget this is to make him simply a servant of man.

Scripture speaks of your pastor as your leader, "who spoke the word of God to you" (Hebrews 13:7). It tells Christians, "Obey your leaders and submit to their authority" (v. 17). Your pastor has authority and can expect obedience from his members, but this does not make him a dictator. He cannot, for instance, demand that the congregation build a church according to a plan he has chosen, or have its services at the time he decides. He can expect obedience only when he speaks the Word of God. Such obedience, then, is not to a human being, but to God, to whom the pastor is also accountable.

But is the pastor in no way accountable to the congregation through whom the Lord called him? Indeed he is, but in a secondary way. Paul commended the Bereans for holding him accountable for what he preached. They "examined the Scriptures every day to see if what Paul said was true" (Acts 17:11). No congregation may permit its pastor to preach or practice contrary to God's Word. A congregation also has the God-given responsibility to act when a called servant no longer is "blameless," no longer is "able to teach," or does not "hold firmly to the trustworthy message." If a pastor, or any called worker, is guilty of immoral conduct or teaching false doctrine, or if there is evident unfaithfulness and incompetence, a congregation may need to terminate his call. In doing this, the congregation in effect also holds him accountable to God.

Ordination / Installation

The pastor you called was a graduate from the seminary. He wrote a letter to your congregation stating that he was accepting your call as a call from the Lord. The pastor who served you during the interim announced that your new pastor would be ordained and installed in an evening service two weeks from Sunday. That is when he would begin his work in your congregation.

The installation reminded you of the inauguration of a president or governor because it marks the time at which the elected or called person begins public service. In the case of the pastor, he at this time promises to conduct his ministry faithfully according to the Scriptures and the Lutheran Confessions. The congregation accepts him as the called servant of Christ, and it is reminded of its duties toward him. The ceremony includes the laying on of hands in prayer. Thus, the ceremony serves to acknowledge the fitness of the person and the validity of the call that has been extended and accepted.

Since your new pastor was a candidate from the seminary entering upon his first call, he was *ordained* and installed. By ordaining him, the church body of which your congregation is a member officially declares him properly trained and qualified to assume the public ministry to which he has been called. He is now listed among its ordained personnel.

This ceremony with the laying on of hands, whether we call it ordination or installation, follows a custom that is briefly described in the New Testament. The seven deacons, Paul and Barnabas as world missionaries, and Timothy as Paul's assistant, began their ministries with a ceremony that included the laying on of hands (Acts 6:6; 13:3; 1 Timothy 4:14). However, no command in Scripture makes ordination or installation or the laying on of hands a divinely prescribed ceremony. The call, as described earlier, establishes the pastor-congregation relationship. Ordination/installation is a ceremony that, in a fitting and orderly manner, marks the beginning of the called person's new ministry.

Roman Catholicism calls ordination the Sacrament of Holy Orders, and only a bishop may perform this sacrament, continuing what is called "apostolic succession." By means of this "sacrament," the bishop appoints an individual as priest and permanently empowers him to perform priestly functions such as celebrating mass, in which, according to Roman Catholic doctrine, the priest changes bread and wine into the body and blood of Christ. Thus, by virtue of ordination, the priest has this permanent position in the church.

We sum up the biblical doctrine in contrast to Rome's teaching:

1. Ordination is not a sacrament, but a church ceremony.

2. Not ordination, but a divine call places an individual
   into the public ministry.

3. Not through the bishop via "apostolic succession,"
   but through a group of Christians or a congregation,
   the Lord calls an individual Christian into the public
   ministry.

4. Not papal authority and church traditions, but only
   the inspired Scriptures must be the source for all
   teachings regarding the public ministry. Since ordination and installation are not commanded or pro-
   hibited in Scripture, the church may in Christian
   freedom determine the purpose and use of this rite in
   the interest of good order.

How gratefully the church will receive those the Lord
gives as its public servants! How prayerfully and conscien-
tiously congregations will go about calling their shepherds
and servants, knowing that it is the Lord in fact who is
calling through them! How faithfully those who have
been called will serve, aware that they are accountable to
their gracious Savior, the Head of the church! In all things
we must do his will and seek his glory.

10

The Ministry: What is the difference?

Traditionally, when the word *minister* was used in a congregation or church body, it referred to the pastor. If someone said, "I am studying for the ministry," it meant he was studying to become a parish pastor. In recent decades the use of the words *minister* and *ministry* has been changing. *Minister* no longer is identified solely with *pastor*. *Ministry*, especially when it is used without the definite article *the*, may refer to a variety of services provided by Christians. "All Christians are ministers and involved in ministry" is the way this is expressed. To avoid confusion, both in our thinking and practice, some distinctions that have already been noted in previous chapters should be emphasized. That is the purpose of this final chapter on the church's ministry.

Terminology

We note again the distinction between *personal ministry* and *public ministry*. The Lord is not speaking to the one and excluding the other when he says, "Make disciples of all nations." He did not entrust the one with the proclamation of the gospel and leave out the other. He gave the gospel equally to all to believe and speak. All equally have been entrusted with the means of grace, the gospel in Word and sacrament. Those in the public ministry are certainly not better Christians than the rest, nor do they constitute an elite group in God's family. The Lord calls all believers priests and kings who are to "declare the praises of him who called you out of darkness into his wonderful light" (1 Peter 2:9). In all of this there is no difference between personal and public *ministry*.

The difference becomes evident in the added terms *personal* and *public*. Both personal and public ministers *minister*, or serve. The former ministers on a personal level as an individual Christian. The latter ministers in a designated office in the name of the *public*, that is, their fellow Christians, through whom the Lord has called them to this *public* service. The following examples illustrate this distinction.

Tom hears that his friend Jim is in the hospital, awaiting serious surgery. As a concerned fellow Christian, he visits Jim, speaks a word of encouragement from Scripture, and prays with him for the Lord's help and blessing. Later, Pastor Smith visits Jim, brings him the comfort of Scripture, prays with him, and gives him private Communion. Pastor Smith does this, not just as a personal friend and fellow Christian, but in the name of the congregation that called him to use the means of grace in its behalf. Through him the congregation is serving Jim. Tom carried out his *personal ministry*; Pastor Smith, the *public ministry* to which he had been called.

Al conducts devotions regularly with his family. He reads from the Scriptures and leads his family in prayer. This is his *personal ministry* in action. Pastor Smith conducts a service: reading Scripture, preaching, and leading the congregation in prayer. The entire congregation as well as visitors are invited to this service. He is doing this for the congregation that called him to this *public ministry*, in their behalf.

Jane is always watching when a new family moves into her neighborhood. Within a few days she stops in to extend a hearty welcome to the new family and inquire about their church membership. Upon hearing that they are looking for a church where their children can go to Sunday school, she tells them about her congregation and about how her children hear about the Savior in Sunday school, and she invites them to send their children. This is her personal ministry in action. She informs Pastor Smith about this new family, and he also visits them. He tells them more about the congregation and the Bible information class he will begin within several weeks. He visits them as the called pastor of the congregation. This is part of his public ministry.

Thus, in our personal ministry we function in our homes, in the world, and in the church on a personal level. In the public ministry a Christian serves as representative of the church and for the church's edification. He is serving in this public manner because the Lord through the church called him to do so. The specific call to public service distinguishes between the two.

Sometimes the terms *pastoral ministry* and *lay ministry*, or *clergy* and *laity*, are used to distinguish between the two.

This can, however, be misleading. The term *clergy* does not include all who are in the public ministry. It refers generally only to parish pastors, or those who have been formally *ordained*, including the thought that they serve on a full-time basis. On the other hand, the term *lay ministry* may be applied to lay members who actually serve in public ministry, although on a limited basis. The following examples illustrate this.

Tom, a lay member of the congregation, has been elected to the board of elders. As such he is asked to visit the Larsens, who seldom attend the worship services. Jim, a neighbor to the Larsens, has personally talked with them about their attendance, but without success. Now Tom, as a member of the congregation's board of elders, shows the congregation's concern. He is going, not only as a personal friend or concerned individual, but in behalf of the congregation. While Jim was carrying out his personal ministry, Tom's visit is part of the congregation's public ministry.

Mary, a mother of two, teaches her children to pray and reads Bible stories to them. This is her personal ministry. She is asked to teach a class in the congregation's Sunday school. She accepts this call from the congregation, and as she carries out this assignment, she is involved in public ministry.

Since Tom and Mary are laypersons, their *public* service sometimes is called *lay ministry*. They were not serving as pastors. On the other hand, what they did in their homes or in their personal ministry may also be referred to as lay ministry. Thus this term is inexact and can be misunderstood.

Similarly, the teacher or principal in the Lutheran elementary school is not called a clergyman, even though his assignment in the public ministry is full-time like the pastor's. Yet he also is not considered to be a layman. He does not fit into either the *clergy* or *lay ministry* category. Thus these terms are not useful in distinguishing between personal and public ministry. *Lay ministry* is ambiguous as to its meaning; *clergy* is too restrictive to be used for the public ministry.

Distinctions within the public ministry

As discussed in a previous chapter, we may distinguish also among the various forms of the public ministry. One distinction we can make is between full-time and part-time public ministries. On the one hand, full-time assignments usually have a broad scope of responsibilities and require extensive training. Among these the most common are pastors, teachers, professors, missionaries, and administrators. As the needs of the church require, it may add staff ministers, youth and evangelism ministers, and the like, who are asked to serve full-time.

On the other hand, part-time assignments are usually more limited in scope and require less specialized training. Examples of these are the members of the board of elders and church council, Sunday school teachers, organists, choir directors, members of a congregation's evangelism committee, and assistants at the distribution of Holy Communion.

All of these are forms of the public ministry. The congregation called these workers to serve in their name, on their behalf. But not all have been called to the same service. In each case the *call* determines how that person is to serve and distinguishes one person's service from another's. Some are given more authority than others. The pastor's call carries with it preaching, teaching, and administrative responsibilities for the entire congregation. A principal's call makes him responsible for the Lutheran elementary school, while a teacher's call assigns a certain class to him or her. An elder may be called to the limited service of helping distribute Holy Communion.

For the sake of good order, the call also outlines the relationships between those who serve the congregation. Some are called to lead and direct and are given the necessary authority, while others may be called to serve under them. It is clear that a teacher must serve under the principal, and the elder under the pastor. Scripture calls on Christians to "obey your leaders and submit to their authority. They keep watch over you as men who must give an account. Obey them so that their work will be a joy, not a burden" (Hebrews 13:17). This does not set up a dictatorship or a hierarchy of power. Those holding positions of responsibility are not to lord it over God's flock entrusted to them. They all are servants under Christ Jesus, their head, and are subject to him and his Word.

Another distinction that is made among those in the public ministry is based on the rite of ordination. Some ministers, such as pastors, have been ordained; others, such as teaching ministers, traditionally have not been ordained. We already discussed ordination and its significance as a church rite not instituted by God. Since the call and not ordination places an individual into the public ministry, ordination does not grant responsibility, power, or privilege in the church that are not inherent in the call. Governments may, however, make distinctions between ordained and nonordained ministers, granting certain tax privileges to the former.

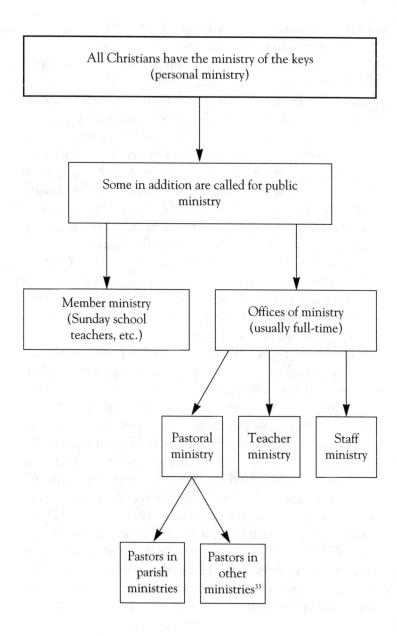

Distinguishing between equipping
for personal and public ministry

When you joined Trinity congregation, you learned much from the pastor's sermons. They spoke to your conscience and exposed sins you ignored or sought to hide and forget. But above all, the pastor comforted your troubled conscience and led you to the Lord Jesus. As the pastor spoke God's Word to you, you heard the Lord Jesus assuring you, "Your sins are forgiven. I give you eternal life." In various ways your pastor carried out his assignment to be a shepherd of "the church of God, which he bought with his own blood" (Acts 20:28). Your faith was nourished with the Bread of Life, your thirst was quenched with the Water of Life. You thanked God for the pastor, the shepherd, he gave you. Your pastor was carrying out the Lord's will, for he says to those who are called as pastors: "Be shepherds of God's flock that is under your care" (1 Peter 5:2).

You learned something else from the pastor's sermons. In many sermons the message and the application encouraged you and equipped you for your personal ministry. You were shown how you could serve your fellow Christians and how you should bring up your children "in the training and instruction of the Lord" (Ephesians 6:4). Your personal ministry of telling others about Jesus was frequently emphasized. In other ways your pastor and teachers followed the Lord's directive to them "to prepare God's people for works of service" (Ephesians 4:12). In Bible class you studied what the Bible says about parenting. You were invited to learn more about evangelism, about telling friends and neighbors about Jesus. The church through its called servants was equipping you for your personal ministry.

Then you were asked to teach one of the Sunday school classes as public service for your congregation. You said: "I don't really know how to do this." You were told: "You can attend special training sessions before you begin, and we'll have regular Sunday school teachers meetings." Thus the congregation will equip those members who are called into some form of public service, as we noted above. The Lord does not expect any Christian to do anything for which he or she is not equipped. The Lord, of course, gives natural gifts, more than we often realize and are ready to use. But he also tells the church to equip Christians for the service to which it calls them. This is particularly true of those who are called into the full-time public ministry. Extensive training is important to qualify individuals to serve as pastors and missionaries and as teachers and professors. We again remember the words of Paul to Timothy: "The things you have heard me say in the presence of many witnesses entrust to reliable men who will also be qualified to teach others" (2 Timothy 2:2). Those who have received such training and are eligible for a call into the full-time public ministry are referred to as candidates for the preaching or teaching ministry. Until they receive a call, they remain laypersons, but their training does set them apart from others who may not be considered qualified for such full-time public service.

Thus, the church may make many distinctions among the servants of God. The distinction between personal and public ministry is one to which the Scripture leads us. In Christian liberty, the church for the sake of good order has made and may make further distinctions. All, however, must be done in the interest of its gospel mission to the glory of God.

Conclusion to Part III

"I'm only a layperson. I can't talk to strangers about Jesus. We called our pastor to do that." "We don't have time for devotions at home. Besides, I'm not good at that. We send our children to Christian day school. The teachers take care of religion for our children." "The congregation asked me to help the pastor distribute Holy Communion. I thought only pastors could do that."

In the family of God, who is to do the work? Who is to serve? Who are ministers? There is really only one answer to those questions: all who are children of God, all Christians; each according to the gifts and call of the Lord.

All who have been brought to faith have a personal ministry in which they carry out the Lord's will to be his witnesses. What a blessing when every Christian reaches out in love to brothers and sisters in Christ and to those outside God's family to bring them in! What a blessing to the church when all serve according to the Lord's will! The sick will be visited, the troubled comforted, sinners brought to repentance, children trained, the gospel spread, unbelievers invited, the Lord ever worshiped. The Lord is praised and the church is blessed when God's people care for and serve one another and their neighbors in personal ministry.

What blessings the Lord has in mind by establishing among his people the public ministry of the Word! May the family of God thank the ascended Head of the church for its faithful pastors, dedicated professors and teachers, able administrators, indeed for all who serve in the various forms of the public ministry. Let all in the church, in its congregations and synods, remember that those "who direct the affairs of the church well are worthy of double honor, especially those whose work is preaching and teaching" (1 Timothy 5:17). Thus, the Lord, who has called them, is praised.

In closing

The church is the family of God. We Christians are this family, united by a common faith in the only Savior from sin, the holy Son of God, the Lord Jesus.

As God's family, we have a mission, given by our Lord and head. "Go! Reach out! Gather my elect into my family of believers. Preach the gospel, through which I make people wise for salvation." As God's family, we have a ministry. As believers, we serve and are served. We are served as the Lord gives us public servants to nurture our faith with the gospel, to inspire Christian living, and to equip us for service. In response to being served, we use our gifts to serve one another in love, serving all people as the Lord gives opportunity in his created world.

Endnotes

[1] Large Catechism, Second Part: The Creed, *The Book of Concord: The Confessions of the Evangelical Lutheran Church*, translated and edited by Theodore G. Tappert (Philadelphia: Fortress Press, 1959), pp. 416,417.

[2] Smalcald Articles III, XII: 2, Tappert, p. 315.

[3] Augsburg Confession, Article VII: 1, Tappert, p. 32.

[4] Apology of the Augsburg Confession, Articles VII and VIII: 5, Tappert, p. 169.

[5] Apology of the Augsburg Confession, Articles VII and VIII: 12, Tappert, p. 170.

[6] Apology of the Augsburg Confession, Articles VII and VIII: 20, Tappert, p. 171.

[7] Apology of the Augsburg Confession, Articles VII and VIII: 28, Tappert, p. 173.

[8] Augsburg Confession, Article VII: 3, Tappert, p. 32.

[9] *Constitution of the Wisconsin Ev. Lutheran Synod*, 1994, Article II, p. 1.

[10] Evangelical Lutheran Church in America, *Confession of Faith*, 2.03.

[11] Evangelical Lutheran Church in America, *Confession of Faith*, 2.05, 2.06.

[12] Solid Declaration of the Formula of Concord, Article VI: 16,17, Tappert, p. 566.

[13] Augsburg Confession, Article XXVIII: 1, Tappert, p. 81.

[14] Augsburg Confession, Article XXVIII: 5, Tappert, p. 81.

[15] Augsburg Confession, Article XXVIII: 10, Tappert, p. 82.

[16]Augsburg Confession, Article XXVIII: 11, Tappert, p. 82.

[17]*The Encyclopedia of the Lutheran Church*, edited by J. Bodensieck (Minneapolis: Augsburg, 1965), Vol. 3, p. 2197.

[18]*Baker Encyclopedia of Psychology*, edited by D. Benner, p. 517.

[19]*Reports and Memorials for the Fifty-second Biennial Convention*, WELS, 1993, p. 209.

[20]*Reports and Memorials*, WELS, 1993, p. 209.

[21]Augsburg Confession, Article V: 2, Tappert, p. 31.

[22]For a complete description and evaluation of the Church Growth Movement, see the following:

Robert Koester, *Law & Gospel: Foundation of Lutheran Ministry* (Milwaukee: Northwestern Publishing House, 1993).

David J. Valleskey, "The Church Growth Movement: An Evaluation," *Wisconsin Lutheran Quarterly*, Vol. 88, No. 2 (1991), pp. 83-123.

Ernst H. Wendland, "An Evaluation of Current Missiology," *Wisconsin Lutheran Quarterly*, Vol. 79, No. 3 (1982), pp. 174-176.

[23]Koester, *Law & Gospel*, p. 172.

[24]Wendland, "An Evaluation," p. 176.

[25]Augsburg Confession, Article V: 1, Tappert, p. 31.

[26]*Doctrinal Statements of the WELS*, 1970, p. 11.

[27]This is the position held by many in the Lutheran Church—Missouri Synod.

[28]Augsburg Confession, Article XIV, Tappert, p. 36.

[29]Martin Luther, *Luther's Works*, American Edition, edited by Jaroslav Pelikan and Helmut T. Lehmann (St. Louis: Concordia Publishing House; Philadelphia: Fortress Press, 1958–1986), Vol. 44, p. 129.

[30]*Luther's Works*, Vol. 26, pp. 17,18.

[31]See A *Bible Study on Man and Woman in God's World*, by John Brug (Milwaukee: Northwestern Publishing House, 1992), for a complete study of the subject.

[32]*Luther's Works*, Vol. 4, p. 204.

[33]Adapted from Thomas P. Nass, "The Pastoral Ministry as a Distinct Form of the Public Ministry," *Wisconsin Lutheran Quarterly*, Vol. 91, No. 4 (1994), p. 258.

For Further Reading

Gawrisch, Wilbert. "The Doctrine of Church and Ministry in the Life of the Church Today." Essay at the Fifty-first Biennial Convention of the Wisconsin Evangelical Lutheran Synod. *Proceedings*, August 1991, pp. 204-247.

Nass, Thomas P. "The Pastoral Ministry as a Distinct Form of the Public Ministry." *Wisconsin Lutheran Quarterly*, Vol. 91, No. 4 (1994), pp. 243-272.

Schuetze, Armin. *Basic Doctrines of the Bible*, ch. 13-15, pp. 80-98. Milwaukee: Northwestern Publishing House, 1986.

"Theses on the Church and Ministry." *Doctrinal Statements of the Wisconsin Evangelical Lutheran Synod*, pp. 3-11. Milwaukee: Northwestern Publishing House, 1970.

WELS Ministry Compendium. Compiled in 1992 by WELS Parish Services. Contains WELS articles on church and ministry from 1869 to 1992.

Scripture Index

Subject Index